Absolute
Predestination

Absolute Predestination

Jerome Zanchius

Sovereign Grace Publishers, Inc.
P.O. Box 4998
Lafayette, IN 47903
2001

Printed In the United States of America
By Lightning Source, Inc.

PUBLISHER'S PREFACE

"Him (Jesus), being delivered up by the determinate counsel and foreknowledge of God, you by wicked hands have crucified and slain"—Acts 2:23

Jesus Christ was predestinated! Is that not a sobering fact to those who deny the doctrine of predestination? Yes, in fact, the Lord of Glory was predestinated to be delivered up to misery, to suffering and to death. By His predetermined counsel and plan, God made certain (*"ordained," "decreed"*) that His beloved and only-begotten Son would be taken by wicked and lawless men who would subject Him to humiliation, shame and death. Furthermore, these wicked men were *"before of old ordained to this condemnation,"*—Jude 4.

Do you believe that? Do you believe that Jesus Christ was born to die? Do you believe that the men who crucified Him were doing the secret will of God, fulfilling God's plan exactly and completely? Do you see that even though these lawless men desired to irreparably frustrate the will of God, thus fulfilling the will and lusts of Satan, they instead fully executed the will of God without deviating from His eternal plan so much as a hairsbreadth? As one scriptural evidence of this, note that they were not permitted to break a bone in His body. Yet this was standard procedure in cases of crucifixion. But God, who not only knows the end from the beginning (but also once and for all time decides the beginning, the end, and all the steps of men between the beginning and the end,) decreed that not a bone should be broken in the body of Jesus. So when God prophecied in the Psalms a thousand years before the crucifixion that none of those precious bones would be broken, He simply revealed something He had before decided and decreed. Do you think He was suspending His reputation for truthfulness upon His ability to persuade willful and wicked human beings at the time of the crucifixion that they should not break the bones of Jesus lest they prove His prophecy wrong and so make Him out a liar? Or do you rather believe God when He says, *"It is not in man to direct his own steps,"* and, *"The ordering of the heart in man and the answer of the tongue is from the Lord"* (Jer. 10:23 and Proverbs 16:1)? Yes, *"A man's heart plans his way, but the LORD directs his steps"* (Proverbs 16:9). It is God's eternal predestination which determines which way every person will make each step.

But some say that a loving, gracious and merciful God could not predestinate the evil acts of men without becoming the author of sin. Does not Acts 2:23 above state plainly that God by His own wise counsel before determined that wicked men should crucify the Lord Jesus? And was not this a horrible, indescribably sinful act toward One who was *"holy, harmless and undefiled"*? If the sinless Son of God might be predestinated to such an undeserved end in order to fulfill the will and plan of God, then how can anyone who deserves shame and pain and death for the thoughts and imaginations of their continually evil hearts (Gen. 6:5) object to the predestination of their acts by a holy, trustworthy and all-wise God?

Jesus was God as well as man, yet He willingly submitted Himself to God's will, His predestinated plan, subjecting His every thought and act to fulfill it. Though Jesus was pure and perfect, yet He was neither too heavenly nor too good to be predestinated to exactly, precisely and without a single self-selected interruption act out God's predestinated plans for His entire life!

JAY GREEN

Jerome Zanchius, Italian reformer, was born February 2, 1516. Bayle's Historical Dictionary states that he was born at Alzano, Italy. But John Sturmius, an intimate friend stated in a speech to the Senate of Strasburgh, March 20, 1562, that Zanchius was born at Bergamo, Italy, a place not too far from Venice.

Zanchius' nobleman father died in the plague of 1528. His mother died just three years later. At this time the fifteen-year-old boy chose to enter a monastery, where he had some relatives. Here he specialized in Aristotle, the languages, and school-divinity for 19 years. Here also he soon became acquainted with Count Celcus Maximian, who also later became a burning light in the Reformation. These two friends lived together sixteen years, pursuing the same studies, finally being blessed with the opportunity to sit under the excellent lectures of Peter Martyr as he expounded the Epistle to the Romans. At the same time Peter Martyr was privately teaching the Psalms to these monks. There is little doubt that the conversion of both Zanchius and Count Maximian occurred under the ministry of the emerging Martyr.

At this time Zanchius reported that he and the Count began to diligently read the Holy Scriptures and to study closely the writings of Augustine and others of the fathers. This continued for several years, during which time they both were preaching publicly more and more the purity and power of the Gospel. In this Count Maximian attained such grace and enlargement of spirit, along with a holy boldness and freedom of utterance that he was forced to flee for his life. The Count finally settled at Geneva, becoming the first pastor of the Protestant Italian Church in that city.

By 1550 Peter Martyr himself was unable to preach in safety, and in that same year that he fled, 18 of his disciples also had to escape from their native land. Among these was Jerome Zanchius. After some time, he also arrived in Geneva, where he remained for nearly 12 months. Then he received an invitation to become divinity professor in England (perhaps at Oxford, where P. Martyr had by then become active). But as he journeyed toward England, he received a counter-invitation to take the divinity chair at Strasburgh, lately vacated by the death of the excellent Caspar Hedio.

Zanchius began to teach at Strasburgh in 1553 and continued to give them excellent instruction for nearly 11 years. But there were some who maliciously persecuted him because of certain of his Biblical beliefs. However, so long as his friend Sturmius remained head of the university, Zanchius found his life there tolerable. At last his carnal-minded enemies broke out in putrefying rancor —Zanchius was then forced to make public defence of his views. It was on October 22, 1562 that he delivered his noted declaration

7

of faith concerning predestination, final perseverance, and the Lord's Supper. Soon his situation grew even more uncomfortable, and he was required to subscribe to the Augsburg Confession or to lose his professorship. This he did with some subscribed limitation. However, it appears certain he had granted too much in regard to Christ's actual presence in the Lord's Supper, causing him pains of conscience thereafter. As usual, a good man's offer to settle the dust of controversy by seeking to find grounds for compromise with his enemies failed to do more than to encourage his persecutors. Though these were Lutherans, they accused Zanchius of heterodoxy in regard to views which Luther himself held (especially in regards to predestination and perseverance).

The beginning of the end of his stay in Strasburgh came when Zanchius moved expertly to block the printing of a book by one Heshusius. This invidius preacher had in his preface wickedly slandered Peter Martyr, Bullinger, Calvin, Zwingli, and many other of the divines God had so largely used in the Reformation. Thus Zanchius, who was undoubtedly a zealous friend to liberty in the publication of religious views, felt compelled to attempt to persuade the magistrates to ban the book. The book was banned, but Heshusius managed to get the book illegally printed. And he used the actions of Zanchius in blocking the legal printing as the final wedge needed to topple him from his post at the University.

Zanchius offered to debate his opponents publicly. They refused to do so. He then went to churches and universities in Germany, obtaining support for his views. This availed nothing. Then at last the Senate of Strasburgh met to consider the views of both sides. They cleared neither, but made up a compromise statement of beliefs which they asked each party to sign. Zanchius did so, but again found it necessary to indicate that he intended to preserve a good conscience and his integrity. Thus he wrote this, "I acknowledge this summary of doctrine to be pious, and so I admit it." No peace followed this effort either. Therefore when an invitation came to him to take the pastorate of the church of Chiavenna, Italy, he obtained the consent of the Senate and of his church to his resignation. During these last years of controversy, he was invited to such famous places as Zurich, Geneva, Leyden, Heidelberg, Marpurg and Lausanne. But at last in November, 1563, he left Strasburgh for Chiavenna.

However, there was no rest waiting for him in Chiavenna, for he had hardly arrived before the town was visited by a pestilential plague that took no less than 1200 inhabitants in 7 months time. Zanchius continued to preach so long as there was an audience, but soon the few survivors were either sick, caring for the sick, or stunned with terror. Finally he took the good advice of friends, withdrawing to a nearby mountaintop residence with his family. After three and a half months he came down from his mountain, resuming his ministry to the stricken town.

In 1567 Frederic III prevailed upon Zanchius to accept a divinity professorship in the University of Heidelberg, following Ursin. In the beginning of the year 1568 he entered on his new duties, and in that same year he received his doctor's degree.

Not long after Frederic III (Elector Palatine) asked Zanchius to write a treatise on the doctrine of the Trinity, particularly begging him to be very particular and explicit in answering the arguments of the Socinians. And notwithstanding a very strong effort by the Socinians to cripple him by flattery, he wrote the two magnificent treatises, *De Dei Natura* and *De Tribus Elohim Uno Eodemque Jehova.*

He held this professorship at Heidelberg for ten years, when, at the death of Frederic III, he chose to take the pastorate of the church at Newstadt, the residence of Prince John Casimir, son of Frederic III. Again at this time he had other attractive offers, one from the University of Leyden, another from the Protestant Church at Antwerp. For 7 years the church at Newstadt basked in the sunlight of this great man's Christian witness, but at last it was necessary for him to retire from the busy pastorate due to the infirmities of age.

The final days of his pilgrimage on earth were spent in the enjoyment of friends at Heidelberg, where on November 19, 1590, God gave him his well-earned reward for a life of faithful service.

The writings of Zanchius made up nine volumes, sometimes bound into three large folios, and these continued to bless the churches of God. Those who read the following treatise on predestination will most likely agree with those who wrote the inscription that appeared on the small monumental stone at the head of Zanchius' grave:

"Here Zanchius rests, whom love of truth constrained
 To quit his own and seek a foreign land.
 How good and great he was, how formed to shine,
 How fraught with science human and divine;
 Sufficient proof his numerous writings give,
 And those who heard him teach and saw him live.
 Earth still enjoys him, though his soul has fled:
 His name is deathless, though his dust is dead."

OBSERVATIONS ON THE DIVINE ATTRIBUTES,

NECESSARY TO BE PREMISED,

IN ORDER TO OUR BETTER UNDERSTANDING THE DOCTRINE OF PREDESTINATION.

ALTHOUGH the great and ever-blessed God is a being absolutely simple and infinitely remote from all shadow of composition, He is, nevertheless, in condescension to our weak and contracted faculties, represented in Scripture as possessed of divers Properties, or Attributes, which, though seemingly different from His Essence, are in reality essential to Him, and constitutive of His very Nature.

Of these attributes, those on which we shall now particularly descant (as being more immediately concerned in the ensuing subject) are the following ones: I., His eternal wisdom and foreknowledge; II., The absolute freedom and liberty of His will; III., The perpetuity and unchangeableness both of Himself and His decrees; IV., His omnipotence; V., His justice; VI., His mercy.

Without an explication of these, the doctrine of Predestination cannot be so well understood, and we shall, therefore, briefly consider them by way of preliminary to the main subject.

THE DIVINE WISDOM AND FOREKNOWLEDGE OF GOD.

I.—With respect to THE DIVINE WISDOM AND FOREKNOWLEDGE, I shall lay down the following positions:—

POSITION 1.—God is, and always was so perfectly

wise, that nothing ever did, or does, or can elude His knowledge. He knew, from all eternity, not only what He Himself intended to do, but also what He would incline and permit others to do. "Known unto God are all His works(ἀπ αἰῶνος)from eternity" (Acts xv. 18).

POSITION 2.—Consequently, God knows nothing now, nor will know anything hereafter, which He did not know and foresee from everlasting, His foreknowledge being co-eternal with Himself, and extending to everything that is or shall be done (Heb. iv. 13). All things, which comprises past, present and future, are naked and open to the eyes of Him with whom we have to do.

POSITION 3.—This foreknowledge of God is not conjectural and uncertain (for then it would not be foreknowledge), but most sure and infallible, so that whatever He foreknows to be future shall necessarily and undoubtedly come to pass. For His knowledge can no more be frustrated, or His wisdom be deceived, than He can cease to be God. Nay, could either of these be the case, He actually would cease to be God, all mistake and disappointment being absolutely incompatible with the Divine nature.

POSITION 4.—The influence which the Divine foreknowledge has on the certain futurition of the things foreknown does not render the intervention of second causes needless, nor destroy the nature of the things themselves.

My meaning is, that the prescience of God does not lay any coercive necessity on the wills of beings naturally free. For instance, man, even in his fallen state, is endued with a natural freedom of will, yet he acts, from the first to the last moment of his life, in absolute subserviency (though, perhaps, he does not know it nor design it) to the purposes and decrees of God concerning him, notwithstanding which, he is sensible of no compulsion, but acts as freely and voluntarily as if he was *sui juris*, subject to no control and absolutely lord of himself. This made Luther,* after he had shown how all

---

* De Serv. Arb. cap. 44.

things necessarily and inevitably come to pass, in consequence of the sovereign will and infallible foreknowledge of God, say that "we should carefully distinguish between a necessity of infallibility and a necessity of coaction, since both good and evil men, though by their actions they fulfil the decree and appointment of God, yet are not forcibly constrained to do any thing, but act willingly."

POSITION 5.—God's foreknowledge, taken abstractedly, is not the sole cause of beings and events, but His will and foreknowledge together. Hence we find (Acts ii. 23) that His determinate counsel and foreknowledge act in concert, the latter resulting from and being founded on the former.

THE WILL OF GOD.

We pass on,

II.—To consider THE WILL OF GOD, with regard to which we assert as follows :—

POSITION 1.—The Deity is possessed not only of infinite knowledge, but likewise of absolute liberty of will, so that whatever He does, or permits to be done, He does and permits freely and of His own good pleasure.

Consequently, it is His free pleasure to permit sin, since, without His permission, neither men nor devils can do anything. Now, to permit is, at least, the same as not to hinder, though it be in our power to hinder if we please, and this permission, or non-hinderance, is certainly an act of the Divine will. Hence Augustine* says, "Those things which, seemingly, thwart the Divine will are, nevertheless, agreeable to it, for, if God did not permit them, they could not be done, and whatever God permits, He permits freely and willingly. He does nothing, neither suffers anything to be done, against His own will." And Luther† observes that "God permitted Adam to fall into sin because He willed that he should so fall."

---

* Enchir. cap. 100. † De Serv. Arb. c. 153.

POSITION 2.—Although the will of God, considered in itself, is simply one and the same, yet, in condescension to the present capacities of man, the Divine will is very properly distinguished into secret and revealed. Thus it was His revealed will that Pharaoh should let the Israelites go, that Abraham should sacrifice his son, and that Peter should not deny Christ; but, as was proved by the event, it was His secret will that Pharaoh should not let Israel go (Exod. iv. 21), that Abraham should not sacrifice Isaac (Gen. xxii. 12), and that Peter should deny his Lord (Matt. xxvi. 34).

POSITION 3.—The will of God, respecting the salvation and condemnation of men, is never contrary to itself; He immutably wills the salvation of the elect and *vice versa;* nor can He ever vary or deviate from His own will in any instance whatever, so as that *that* should be done, which He willeth not, or *that* not be brought to pass, which He willeth. " My counsel shall stand, and I will do all My pleasure " (Isa. xlvi. 10). " The counsel of the Lord standeth for ever, and the thoughts of His heart to all generations " (Psalm xxxiii. 11). " He is in one mind, and who can turn Him? and what His soul desireth, even that He doeth. For He performeth the thing that is appointed for me : and many such things are with Him " (Job xxiii. 13, 14). " Being predestinated according to the purpose of Him who worketh all things after the counsel of His own will " (Eph. i. 11).

Thus, for instance, Hophni and Phineas hearkened not to the voice of their father, who reproved them for their wickedness, because the Lord *would* slay them (1 Sam. ii. 25), and Sihon, king of Heshbon, would not receive the peaceable message sent him by Moses because the Lord God hardened his spirit, and made his heart obstinate, that He might deliver him into the hand of Israel (Deut. ii. 26, 30). Thus also, to add no more, we find that there have been, and ever will be, some whose eyes God blindeth, and whose hearts He hardeneth, *i.e.,* whom God permits to continue blind and hardened on

purpose to prevent their seeing with their eyes and understanding with their hearts, and to hinder their conversion
to God and spiritual healing by Him (Isa. vi. 9; John
xii. 39, 40).

POSITION 4.—Because God's will of precept may, in
some instances, appear to thwart His will of determination, it does not follow either (1) that He mocks His
creatures, or (2) that they are excusable for neglecting to
observe His will of command.

(1) He does not hereby mock His creatures, for if
men do not believe His word nor observe His precepts,
the fault is not in Him, but in themselves; their unbelief
and disobedience are not owing to any ill infused into
them by God, but to the vitiosity of their depraved nature
and the perverseness of their own wills.   Now, if God
invited all men to come to Him, and then shut the door
of mercy against any who were desirous of entering, His
invitation would be a mockery and unworthy of Himself;
but we insist on it, that He does not invite all men to
come to Him in a saving way, and that every individual
person who is, through His gracious influence on his
heart, made willing to come to Him, shall sooner or later
be surely saved by Him, and that with an everlasting
salvation.

(2) Man is not excusable for neglecting God's will of
command. Pharaoh was faulty, and therefore justly
punishable, for not obeying God's revealed will, though
God's secret will rendered that obedience impossible.
Abraham would have committed sin had he refused to
sacrifice Isaac, and in looking to God's secret will would
have acted counter to His revealed one. So Herod,
Pontius Pilate, and the reprobate Jews were justly condemned for putting *Christ* to death, inasmuch as it was
a most notorious breach of God's revealed will. "Thou
shalt do no murder," yet, in slaying the Messiah, they
did no more than God's hand and His counsel—*i.e.*, His
secret, ordaining will—determined before should be done
(Acts iv. 27, 28); and Judas is justly punished for per-

fidiously and wickedly betraying Christ, though his perfidy and wickedness were (but not with his design) subservient to the accomplishment of the decree and word of God.

The brief of the matter is this : secret things belong to God, and those that are revealed belong to us ; therefore, when we meet with a plain precept, we should simply endeavour to obey it, without tarrying to inquire into God's hidden purpose. Venerable Bucer, after taking notice how God hardened Pharaoh's heart, and making some observations on the apostle's simile of a potter and his clay, adds* that "Though God has at least the same right over His creatures, and is at liberty to make them what He will and direct them to the end that pleaseth Himself, according to His sovereign and secret determination, yet it by no means follows that they do not act freely and spontaneously, or that the evil they commit is to be charged on God."

POSITION 5.—God's hidden will is peremptory and absolute, and therefore cannot be hindered from taking effect. God's will is nothing else than God Himself willing, consequently it is omnipotent and unfrustrable. Hence we find it termed by Augustine and the schoolmen, *voluntus omnipotentissima*, because whatever God wills cannot fail of being effected. This made Augustine say,† "Evil men do many things contrary to God's revealed will, but so great is His wisdom, and so inviolable His truth, that He directs all things into those channels which He foreknew." And again,‡ "No free will of the creature can resist the will of God, for man cannot so will or nill as to obstruct the Divine determination or overcome the Divine power." Once more,§ "It cannot be questioned but God does all things, and ever did, according to His own purpose : the human will cannot resist Him so as to make Him do more or less than it is His pleasure to do ; *quandoquidem etiam de ipsis hominum voluntatibus*

---

* Bucer ad Rom. ix. † De Civ. Dei. l. 22, c. 1, Vol. 2, p. 474, T. T. Clark's Edition. ‡ De Corr. and Grat. c. 14.
§ De Corr. and Grat. 14.

quod vult facit, since He does what He pleases even with the wills of men."

POSITION 6.—Whatever comes to pass, comes to pass by virtue of this absolute omnipotent will of God, which is the primary and supreme cause of all things. " Thou hast created all things, and for Thy pleasure they are and were created " (Rev. iv. 11). "Our God is in the heavens ; He hath done whatsoever He hath pleased " (Psa. cxv. 3). " He doeth according to His will, in the army of heaven, and among the inhabitants of the earth ; and none can stay His hand, or say unto Him, What doest Thou? " (Dan. iv. 35). " Whatsoever the Lord pleased, that did He in heaven, and in earth, in the seas, and all deep places " (Psa. cxxxv. 6). "Are not two sparrows sold for a farthing? and one of them shall not fall to the ground without your Father " (Matt. x. 29). To all which Augustine* subscribes when he says, " Nothing is done but what the Almighty wills should be done, either efficiently or permissively." As does Luther, whose words are these,† " This therefore must stand ; to wit, the unsearchable will of God, without which nothing exists or acts." And again (c. 160), "God would not be such if He was not almighty, and if anything could be done without Him." And elsewhere (c. 158) he quotes these words of Erasmus : " Supposing there was an earthly prince, who could do whatever he would and none were able to resist him, we might safely say of such an one that he would certainly fulfil his own desire ; in like manner the will of God, which is the first cause of all things, should seem to lay a kind of necessity upon our wills." This Luther approves of, and subjoins, " Thanks be to God for this orthodox passage in Erasmus's discourse ! But if this be true, what becomes of his doctrine of free-will, which he, at other times, so strenuously contends for? "

POSITION 7.—The will of God is so the cause of all things, as to be itself without cause, for nothing can be

---

* Tom. 3 in Enchir.   † De Serv. Arb. c. 143.

the cause of that which is the cause of everything. So that the Divine will is the *ne plus ultra* of all our inquiries ; when we ascend to that, we can go no farther. Hence we find every matter resolved ultimately into the mere sovereign pleasure of God, as the spring and occasion of whatsoever is done in heaven and earth. "Thou hast hid these things from the wise and prudent, and hast revealed them unto babes : even so, Father, for so it seemed good in Thy sight " (Matt. xi. 25). " It is your Father's good pleasure to give you the kingdom " (Luke xii. 32). " I will, be thou clean " (Matt. viii. 3). " He went up into a mountain, and called unto Him whom He would " (Mark iii. 13). "Of His own will begat He us, with the word of truth " (James i. 18). " Which were born not of blood, nor of the will of the flesh, nor of the will of man, but of God " (John i. 13). " I will have mercy on whom I will have mercy, and I will have compassion on whom I will have compassion. Therefore, He hath mercy on whom He will have mercy, and whom He will He hardeneth " (Rom. ix. 15, 18). And no wonder that the will of God should be the main spring that sets all inferior wheels in motion, and should likewise be the rule by which He goes in all His dealings with His creatures, since nothing out of God (*i.e.*, exterior to Himself) can possibly induce Him to will or nill one thing rather than another. Deny this, and you, at one stroke, destroy His immutability and independency, since He can never be independent, who acts *pro re nata*, as emergency requires, and whose will is suspended on that of others ; nor unchangeable whose purposes vary, and take all shapes, according as the persons or things vary, who are the objects of those purposes. The only reason, then, that can be assigned *why* the Deity does this or omits that is because it is His own free pleasure. Luther,* in answer to that question, " Whence it was that Adam was permitted to fall and corrupt his whole posterity, when God could have prevented his falling,"

---

* De Serv. Arb. c. 153.

etc., says : "God is a Being, whose will acknowledges no cause, neither is it for us to prescribe rules to His sovereign pleasure, or call Him to account for what He does. He has neither superior nor equal, and His will is the rule of all things. He did not therefore will such and such things because they were in themselves right, and He was bound to will them ; but they are therefore equitable and right because He wills them. The will of man, indeed, may be influenced and moved, but God's will never can. To assert the contrary is to undeify Him." Bucer* likewise observes : "God has no other motive for what He does than *ipsa voluntas*, His own mere will, which will is so far from being unrighteous that it is justice itself."

POSITION 8.—Since, as was lately observed, the determining will of God being omnipotent cannot be obstructed or made void, it follows that He never did, nor does He now, will that every individual of mankind should be saved. If this was His will, not one single soul could ever be lost (for who hath resisted His will?), and He would surely afford all men those effectual means of salvation, without which it cannot be had. Now, God could afford these means as easily to all mankind as to some only, but experience proves that He does not ; and the reason is equally plain, namely, that He will not, for whatsoever the Lord pleaseth, that does He in heaven and on earth. It is said, indeed, by the apostle, that God " would have all men saved, and come to the knowledge of the truth," *i.e.*, as Augustine,† consistently with other Scriptures, explains the passage, "God will save some out of the whole race of mankind," that is, persons of all nations, kindreds and tongues. Nay, He will save all men, *i.e.*, as the same father observes, " Every kind of men, or men of every kind," namely, the whole election of grace, be they bond or free, noble or ignoble, rich or poor, male or female. Add to this that it evidently militates against the majesty, omnipotence and supremacy

---

* Ad Rom. ix.   † Enchir. c. 103 and De Cor. and Gr. c. 14.

of God to suppose that He can either will anything in vain, or that anything can take effect against His will; therefore Bucer observes, very rightly (ad Rom. ix.), "God doth not will the salvation of reprobates, seeing He hath not chosen them, neither created them to that end." Consonant to which are those words of Luther,* "This mightily offends our rational nature, that God should, of His own mere unbiassed will, leave some men to themselves, harden them, and then condemn them; but He has given abundant demonstration, and does continually, that this is really the case, namely, that the sole cause why some are saved and others perish proceeds from His willing the salvation of the former and the perdition of the latter, according to that of Paul, 'He hath mercy on whom He will have mercy, and whom He will He hardeneth.'"

POSITION 9.—As God doth not will that each individual of mankind should be saved, so neither did He will that Christ should properly and immediately die for each individual of mankind, whence it follows that, though the blood of Christ, from its own intrinsic dignity, was sufficient for the redemption of all men, yet, in consequence of His Father's appointment, He shed it intentionally, and therefore effectually and immediately, for the elect only.

This is self-evident. God, as we have before proved, wills not the salvation of every man, but He gave His Son to die for them whose salvation He willed; therefore His Son did not die for every man. All those for whom Christ died are saved, and the Divine justice indispensably requires that to them the benefits of His death should be imparted; but only the elect are saved, they only partake of those benefits, consequently for them only He died and intercedes. The apostle (Rom. viii.) asks, "Who shall lay anything to the charge of God's elect? it is God that justifies," *i.e.*, His elect, exclusively of others; "who is He that condemneth? It is Christ that died"

---

* De Serv. Arb. c. 161.

for them, exclusive of others. The plain meaning of the passage is that those whom God justifies, and for whom Christ died (justification and redemption being of exactly the same extent), cannot be condemned. These privileges are expressly restrained to the elect : therefore God justifies and Christ died for them alone.

In the same chapter Paul asks, " He that spared not His own Son, but delivered Him up for us all [*i.e.*, for all us elect persons], how shall He not, with Him, also freely give us all things? " *i.e.*, salvation and all things necessary to it. Now, it is certain that these are not given to every individual, and yet, if Paul says true, they are given to all those for whom Christ was delivered to death; consequently He was not delivered to death for every individual. To the same purpose Augustine argues in Johan. tract. 45, col. 335. Hence that saying of Ambrose,* *"si non credis non tibi passus est, i.e.*, if you are an unbeliever, Christ did not die for you." Meaning that whoever is left under the power of final unbelief is thereby evidenced to be one of those for whom Christ did not die, but that all for whom He suffered shall be, in this life, sooner or later, indued with faith. The Church of Smyrna, in their letter to the dioceses of Pontus, insist everywhere on the doctrine of special redemption.† Bucer, in all parts of his works, observes that "Christ died restrictively for the elect only, but for them universally."

POSITION 10.—From what has been laid down, it follows that Augustine, Luther, Bucer, the scholastic divines, and other learned writers are not to be blamed for asserting that "God may in some sense be said to will the being and commission of sin." For, was this contrary to His determining will of permission, either He would not be omnipotent, or sin could have no place in the world; but He is omnipotent, and sin has a place in the world, which it could not have if God willed otherwise; for who hath resisted His will? (Rom. ix.). No

---

* Ambros. Tom. 2 de fid, ad Grat. l. 4, c. i.
† Vid. Euseb. Hist. l. 4, c. 10.

one can deny that God permits sin, but He neither permits it ignorantly nor unwillingly, therefore knowingly and willingly (vide Aust. Enchir. c. 96). Luther stedfastly maintains this in his book de Serv. Arbitr. and Bucer in Rom. i. However, it should be carefully noticed : (1) That God's permission of sin does not arise from His taking delight in it ; on the contrary, sin, as sin, is the abominable thing that His soul hateth, and His efficacious permission of it is for wise and good purposes. Whence that observation of Augustine,* "God, who is no less omnipotent than He is supremely and perfectly holy, would never have permitted evil to enter among His works, but in order that He might do good even with that evil," *i.e.*, over-rule it for good in the end. (2) That God's free and voluntary permission of sin lays no man under any forcible or compulsive necessity of committing it ; consequently the Deity can by no means be termed the author of moral evil, to which He is not, in the proper sense of the word, accessory, but only remotely or negatively so, inasmuch as He could, if He pleased, absolutely prevent it.

We should, therefore, be careful not to give up the omnipotence of God under a pretence of exalting His holiness ; He is infinite in both, and therefore neither should be set aside or obscured. To say that God absolutely nills the being and commission of sin, while experience convinces us that sin is acted every day, is to represent the Deity as a weak, impotent being, who would fain have things go otherwise than they do, but cannot accomplish His desire. On the other hand, to say that He willeth sin doth not in the least detract from the holiness and rectitude of His nature, because, whatever God wills, as well as whatever He does, cannot be eventually evil : materially evil it may be, but, as was just said, it must ultimately be directed to some wise and just end, otherwise He could not will it ; for His will is

---

* Enchir. c. 11.

righteous and good, and the sole rule of right and wrong, as is often observed by Augustine, Luther and others.

POSITION 11.—In consequence of God's immutable will and infallible foreknowledge, whatever things come to pass, come to pass necessarily, though with respect to second causes and us men, many things are contingent, *i.e.*, unexpected and seemingly accidental.

That this was the doctrine of Luther, none can deny who are in any measure acquainted with his works, particularly with his treatise, " De Servo Arbitrio, or Free-will a Slave," the main drift of which book is to prove that the will of man is by nature enslaved to evil only, and, because it is fond of that slavery, is therefore said to be free. Among other matters, he proves there that " whatever man does, he does necessarily, though not with any sensible compulsion, and that we can only do what God from eternity willed and foreknew we should, which will of God must be effectual and His foresight must be certain." Hence we find him saying,* " It is most necessary and salutary for a Christian to be assured that God foreknows nothing uncertainly, but that He determines, and foresees, and acts in all things according to His own eternal, immutable and infallible will," adding, " Hereby, as with a thunderbolt, is man's free-will thrown down and destroyed." A little after, he shows in what sense he took the word " necessity." " By it," says he, " I do not mean that the will suffers any forcible constraint or co-action, but the infallible accomplishment of those things which the immutable God decreed and foreknew concerning us." He goes on : " Neither the Divine nor human will does anything by constraint, but whatever man does, be it good or bad, he does with as much appetite and willingness as if his will was really free. But, after all, the will of God is certain and unalterable, and is the governess of ours."

Exactly consonant to all which are those words of Luther's friend and fellow-labourer, Melancthon† : "All

---

* Cap. 17, in Resp. ad præf.   † In Eph. 1.

things turn out according to Divine predestination, not only the works we do outwardly, but even the thoughts we think inwardly," adding, in the same place, "There is no such thing as chance or fortune, nor is there a readier way to gain the fear of God, and to put our whole trust in Him, than to be thoroughly versed in the doctrine of predestination." I could cite, to the same purpose, Augustine, Aquinas, and many other learned men, but, for brevity's sake, forbear. That this is the doctrine of Scripture every adept in those sacred books cannot but acknowledge. See particularly Psalm cxxxv. 6; Matt. x. 29; Prov. xvi. 1; Matt. xxvi. 54; Luke xxii. 22; Acts iv. 28; Eph. i. 11; Isa. xlvi. 10.

POSITION 12.—As God knows nothing now which He did not know from all eternity, so He wills nothing now which He did not will from everlasting.

This position needs no explanation nor enforcement, it being self-evident that if anything can accede to God *de novo, i.e.*, if He can at any time be wiser than He always was, or will that at one time which He did not will from all eternity, these dreadful consequences must ensue : (1) That the knowledge of God is not perfect, since what is absolutely perfect *non recipit magis et minus* cannot admit either of addition or detraction. If I add to anything, it is from a supposal that that thing was not complete before; if I detract from it, it is supposed that that detraction renders it less perfect than it was. But the knowledge of God, being infinitely perfect, cannot, consistently with that perfection, be either increased or lessened. (2) That the will of God is fluctuating, mutable and unsteady; consequently, that God Himself is so, His will coinciding with His essence, contrary to the avowed assurances of Scripture and the strongest dictates of reason, as we shall presently show when we come to treat of the Divine immutability.

POSITION 13.—The absolute will of God is the original spring and efficient cause of His people's salvation.

I say the original and efficient, for, *sensu complexo,*

there are other intermediate causes of their salvation, which, however, all result from and are subservient to this primary one, the will of God. Such are His everlasting choice of them to eternal life—the eternal covenant of grace, entered into by the Trinity, in behalf of the elect; the incarnation, obedience, death and intercession of Christ for them—all which are so many links in the great chain of causes, and not one of these can be taken away without marring and subverting the whole Gospel plan of salvation by Jesus Christ. We see, then, that the free, unbiassed, sovereign will of God is the root of this tree of life, which bears so many glorious branches and yields such salutary fruits : He therefore loved the elect and ordained them to life because He would ; according to that of the apostle, "having predestinated us, according to the good pleasure of His will" (Eph. i. 5). Then, next after God's covenant for His people and promises to them, comes in the infinite merit of Christ's righteousness and atonement, for we were chosen to salvation in Him as members of His mystic body, and through Him, as our Surety and Substitute, by whose vicarious obedience to the moral law and submission to its curse and penalty, all we, whose names are in the book of life, should never incur the Divine hatred or be punished for our sins, but continue to eternity, as we were from eternity, heirs of God and joint-heirs with Christ. But still the Divine grace and favour (and God extends these to whom He will) must be considered as what gave birth to the glorious scheme of redemption, according to what our Lord Himself teaches us, "God so loved the world, that He gave His only-begotten Son," etc. (John iii. 16), and that of the apostle, "In this was manifested the love of God towards us, because that He sent His only-begotten Son into the world, that we might live through Him" (1 John iv. 9).

POSITION 14.—Since this absolute will of God is both immutable and omnipotent, we infer that the salvation of every one of the elect is most infallibly certain, and can by no means be prevented. This necessarily follows from what we have already asserted and proved concerning the Divine will, which, as it cannot be disappointed or made void, must undoubtedly secure the salvation of all whom God wills should be saved.

From the whole of what has been delivered under this second head, I would observe that the genuine tendency of these truths is not to make men indolent and careless, or lull them to sleep on the lap of presumption and carnal security, but (1) to fortify the people of Christ against the attacks of unbelief and the insults of their spiritual enemies. And what is so fit, to guard them against these, as the comfortable persuasion of God's unalterable will to save them, and of their unalienable interest in the sure mercies of David? (2) To withdraw them entirely from all dependence whether on themselves or any creature whatever; to make them renounce their own righteousness, no less than their sins, in point of reliance, and to acquiesce sweetly and safely in the certain perpetuity of His rich favour. (3) To excite them, from a trust of His goodwill toward them, to love that God who hath given such great and numberless proofs of His love to men, and, in all their thoughts, words and works, to aim, as much as possible, at His honour and glory.

We were to consider—

THE UNCHANGEABLENESS OF GOD AND HIS DECREES.

III.—THE UNCHANGEABLENESS, WHICH IS ESSENTIAL TO HIMSELF AND HIS DECREES.

POSITION 1.—God is essentially unchangeable in Himself. Were He otherwise, He would be confessedly imperfect, since whoever changes must change either for the better or for the worse; whatever alteration any being undergoes, that being must, *ipso facto*, either become more excellent than it was or lose some of the excellency which it had. But neither of these can be the case with

the Deity : He cannot change for the better, for that
would necessarily imply that He was not perfectly good
before ; He cannot change for the worse, for then He
could not be perfectly good after that change. Ergo,
God is unchangeable. And this is the uniform voice of
Scripture. "I am the Lord, I change not" (Mal. iii. 6).
"With Him is no variableness, neither shadow of turn-
ing" (James i. 17). "Thou art the same, and Thy years
shall have no end" (Psalm cii. 27).

POSITION 2.—God is likewise absolutely unchangeable
with regard to His purposes and promises. "God is not
a man, that He should lie ; neither the son of man, that
He should repent : hath He said, and shall He not do it?
or, hath He spoken, and shall He not make it good?"
(Numb. xxiii. 19). "The Strength of Israel will not lie,
nor repent ; for He is not a man, that He should repent"
(1 Sam. xv. 29). "He is in one mind, and who can
turn Him?" (Job xxiii. 13). "I, the Lord, have spoken
it, it shall come to pass, and I will do it ; I will not go
back, neither will I spare, neither will I repent" (Ezek.
xxiv. 14). "The gifts and calling of God are without
repentance" (Rom. xi. 29). "He abideth faithful, and
cannot deny Himself" (2 Tim. ii. 13).

By the purpose or decree of God, we mean His determinate counsel, whereby He did from all eternity pre-
ordain whatever He should do, or would permit to be
done, in time. In particular, it signifies His everlasting
appointment of some men to life, and of others to death,
which appointment flows entirely from His own free and
sovereign will. "The children not yet being born, neither
having done any good or evil (that the purpose of God,
according to election, might stand, not of works, but of
Him that calleth), it was said, the elder shall serve the
younger : as it is written, Jacob have I loved, but Esau
have I hated" (Rom. ix. 11).

The apostle, then, in the very next words, anticipates
an objection, which he foresaw men of corrupt minds
would make to this, "What shall we say then? is there

unrighteousness with God?" which he answers with, "God forbid!" and resolves the whole of God's procedure with His creatures into His own sovereign and independent will, for He said to Moses, "I will have mercy on whom I will have mercy, and I will have compassion on whom I will have compassion."

We assert that the decrees of God are not only immutable as to Himself, it being inconsistent with His nature to alter in His purposes or change His mind; but that they are immutable likewise with respect to the objects of those decrees, so that whatsoever God hath determined, concerning every individual person or thing, shall surely and infallibly be accomplished in and upon them. Hence we find that He actually showeth mercy on whom He decreed to show mercy, and hardeneth whom He resolved to harden (Rom. ix. 18); "For His counsel shall stand, and He will do all His pleasure" (Isa. xlvi. 10). Consequently, His eternal predestination of men and things must be immutable as Himself, and, so far from being reversible, can never admit of the least variation.

POSITION 3.—"Although," to use the words of Gregory, "God never swerves from His decree, yet He often varies in His declarations": that is always sure and immoveable; these are sometimes seemingly discordant. So when He gave sentence against the Ninevites by Jonah, saying, "Yet forty days, and Nineveh shall be overthrown," the meaning of the words is not that God absolutely intended, at the end of that space, to destroy the city, but that, should God deal with those people according to their deserts, they would be totally extirpated from the earth, and should be so extirpated unless they repented speedily.

Likewise, when He told King Hezekiah by the prophet Isaiah, "Set thine house in order, for thou shalt die and not live," the meaning was that with respect to second causes, and, considering the king's bad state of health and emaciated constitution, he could not, humanly speaking, live much longer. But still the event showed that God had immutably determined that he should live fifteen years more, and in order to that had put it into his heart to pray for the blessing decreed, just as, in the case of Nineveh, lately mentioned, God had resolved not to overthrow that city then; and, in order to the accomplishment of His own purpose in a way worthy of Himself, made the ministry of Jonah the means of leading that people to repentance. All which, as it shows that God's absolute predestination does not set aside the use of means, so does it likewise prove that, however various the declarations of God may appear (to wit, when they proceed on a regard had to natural causes), His counsels and designs stand firm and immovable, and can neither admit of alteration in themselves, nor of hindrance in their execution. See this farther explained by Bucer in Rom. ix., where you will find the certainty of the Divine appointment solidly asserted and unanswerably vindicated.

THE OMNIPOTENCE OF GOD.

IV.—We now come to consider THE OMNIPOTENCE OF GOD.

POSITION 1.—God is, in the most unlimited and absolute sense of the word, Almighty. "Behold Thou hast made the heaven and the earth by Thy great power and stretched-out arm, and there is nothing too hard for Thee" (Jer. xxxii. 17). "With God all things are possible" (Matt. xix. 26). The schoolmen, very properly, distinguish the omnipotence of God into absolute and actual: by the former, God might do many things which He does not; by the latter, He actually does whatever He will. For instance, God might, by virtue of His absolute power, have made more worlds than He has. He might have eternally saved every individual of mankind, without reprobating any; on the other hand, He might, and that with the strictest justice, have condemned all men and saved none. He could, had it been

His pleasure, have prevented the fall of angels and men, and thereby have hindered sin from having footing in and among His creatures. By virtue of His actual power He made the universe; executes the whole counsel of His will, both in heaven and earth; governs and influences both men and things, according to His own pleasure; fixes the bounds which they shall not pass, and, in a word, worketh all in all (Isa. xlv. 7; Amos iii. 6; John v. 17; Acts xvii. 26; 1 Cor. xii. 6).

POSITION 2.—Hence it follows that, since all things are subject to the Divine control, God not only works efficaciously on His elect, in order that they may will and do that which is pleasing in His sight, but does, likewise, frequently and powerfully suffer the wicked to fill up the measure of their iniquities by committing fresh sins. Nay, He sometimes, but for wise and gracious ends, permits His own people to transgress, for He has the hearts and wills of all men in His own hand, and inclines them to good or delivers them up to evil, as He sees fit, yet without being the author of sin, as Luther, Bucer, Augustine, and others have piously and Scripturally taught.

This position consists of two parts: (1) That God efficaciously operates on the hearts of His elect, and is thereby the sole Author of all the good they do. (See Eph. iii. 20; Phil. ii. 13; 1 Thess. ii. 13; Heb. xiii. 21.) St. Augustine* takes up no fewer than nineteen chapters in proving that whatever good is in men, and whatever good they are enabled to do, is solely and entirely of God, who, says he, " works in holy persons all their good desires, their pious thoughts, and their righteous actions; and yet these holy persons, though thus wrought upon by God, will and do all these things freely, for it is He who rectifies their wills, which, being originally evil, are made good by Him, and which wills, after He hath set them right and made them good, He directs to good

---

* De Grat. and lib. Arb. a c. 1. usque ad c. 20.

actions and to eternal life, wherein He does not force their wills, but makes them willing."

(2) That God often lets the wicked go on to more ungodliness, which He does (a) negatively by withholding that grace which alone can restrain them from evil; (b) remotely, by the providential concourse and mediation of second causes, which second causes, meeting and acting in concert with the corruption of the reprobate's unregenerate nature, produce sinful effects; (c) judicially, or in a way of judgment. "The King's heart is in the hand of the Lord, as the rivers of waters; He turneth it whithersoever He will" (Prov. xxi. 1); and if the King's heart, why not the hearts of all men? "Out of the mouth of the Most High proceedeth not evil and good?" (Lam. iii. 38). Hence we find that the Lord bid Shimei curse David (2 Sam. xvi. 10); that He moved David himself to number the people (compare 1 Chron. xxi. 1 with 2 Sam. xxiv. 1); stirred up Joseph's brethren to sell him into Egypt (Genesis l. 20); positively and immediately hardened the heart of Pharaoh (Exod. iv. 21); delivered up David's wives to be defiled by Absalom (2 Sam. xii. 11; xvi. 22); sent a lying spirit to deceive Ahab (1 Kings xxii. 20-23), and mingled a perverse spirit in the midst of Egypt, that is, made that nation perverse, obdurate and stiff-necked (Isa. xix. 14). To cite other instances would be almost endless, and after these, quite unnecessary, all being summed up in that express passage, "I make peace and create evil; I the Lord do all these things" (Isa. xlv. 7). See farther, 1 Sam. xvi. 14; Psalm cv. 25; Jer. xiii. 12, 13; Acts ii. 23, iv. 28; Rom. xi. 8; 2 Thess. ii. 11, every one of which implies more[*] than a bare permission of sin. Bucer asserts this, not only in the place referred to below, but continually throughout his works, particularly on Matt. vi. § 2, where this is the sense of his comments on that petition, "Lead us not into temptation": "It is abundantly evident,

---

[*] Vid. Augustin. de Grat. and lib. Arbitr. c. 20 and 21, and Bucer in Rom. 1 sect. 7.

THE OMNIPOTENCE OF GOD.

from most express testimonies of Scripture, that God, occasionally in the course of His providence, puts both elect and reprobate persons into circumstances of temptation, by which temptation are meant not only those trials that are of an outward, afflictive nature, but those also that are inward and spiritual, even such as shall cause the persons so tempted actually to turn aside from the path of duty, to commit sin, and involve both themselves and others in evil. Hence we find the elect complaining, 'O Lord, why hast Thou made us to err from Thy ways, and hardened our hearts from Thy fear?' (Isaiah lxiii. 17). But there is also a kind of temptation, which is peculiar to the non-elect, whereby God, in a way of just judgment, makes them totally blind and obdurate, inasmuch as they are vessels of wrath fitted to destruction." (See also his exposition of Rom. ix.)

Luther* reasons to the very same effect; some of his words are these : " It may seem absurd to human wisdom that God should harden, blind and deliver up some men to a reprobate sense—that He should first deliver them over to evil, and then condemn them for that evil—but the believing spiritual man sees no absurdity at all in this, knowing that God would be never a whit less good, even though He should destroy all men." And again, "God worketh all things in all men, even wickedness in the wicked, for this is one branch of His own omnipotence." He very properly explains how God may be said to harden men, etc., and yet not be the author of their sin. " It is not to be understood," says he, " as if God found men good, wise and tractable, and then made them wicked, foolish and obdurate; but God, finding them depraved, judicially and powerfully excites them just as they are (unless it is His will to regenerate any of them), and, by thus exciting them, they become more blind and obstinate than they were before." (See this whole subject debated at large in the places last referred to.)

POSITION 3.—God, as the primary and efficient cause

* De Serv. Arb. c. 8 and 146 and 147, usq. ad c. 165.

of all things, is not only the Author of those actions done by His elect as actions, but also as they are good actions, whereas, on the other hand, though He may be said to be the Author of all the actions done by the wicked, yet He is not the Author of them in a moral and compound sense as they are sinful; but physically, simply and *sensu diviso* as they are mere actions, abstractedly from all consideration of the goodness or badness of them.

Although there is no action whatever which is not in some sense either good or bad, yet we can easily conceive of an action, purely as such, without adverting to the quality of it, so that the distinction between an action itself and its denomination of good or evil is very obvious and natural.

In and by the elect, therefore, God not only produces works and actions through His almighty power, but likewise, through the salutary influences of His Spirit, first makes their persons good, and then their actions so too; but, in and by the reprobate, He produces actions by His power alone, which actions, as neither issuing from faith nor being wrought with a view to the Divine glory, nor done in the manner prescribed by the Divine Word, are, on these accounts, properly denominated evil. Hence we see that God does not, immediately and *per se*, infuse iniquity into the wicked; but, as Luther expresses it, powerfully excites them to action, and withholds those gracious influences of His Spirit, without which every action is necessarily evil. That God either directly or remotely excites bad men as well as good ones to action cannot be denied by any but Atheists, or by those who carry their notions of free-will and human independency so high as to exclude the Deity from all actual operation in and among His creatures, which is little short of Atheism. Every work performed, whether good or evil, is done in strength and by the power derived immediately from God Himself, "in whom all men live, move, and have their being" (Acts xvii. 28). As, at first, without Him was not anything made which was made, so, now, without Him is not anything done which is done. We have no power or faculty, whether corporal or intellectual, but what we received from God, subsists by Him, and is exercised in subserviency to His will and appointment. It is He who created, preserves, actuates and directs all things. But it by no means follows, from these premises, that God is therefore the cause of sin, for sin is nothing but ἀνομία, illegality, want of conformity to the Divine law (1 John iii. 4), a mere privation of rectitude; consequently, being itself a thing purely negative, it can have no positive or efficient cause, but only a negative and deficient one, as several learned men have observed.

Every action, as such, is undoubtedly good, it being an actual exertion of those operative powers given us by God for that very end; God therefore may be the Author of all actions (as He undoubtedly is), and yet not be the Author of evil. An action is constituted evil three ways—by proceeding from a wrong principle, by being directed to a wrong end, and by being done in a wrong manner. Now, though God, as we have said, is the efficient cause of our actions as actions, yet, if these actions commence sinful, that sinfulness arises from ourselves. Suppose a boy, who knows not how to write, has his hand guided by his master and nevertheless makes false letters, quite unlike the copy set him, though his preceptor, who guides his hand, is the cause of his writing at all, yet his own ignorance and unskilfulness are the cause of his writing so badly. Just so, God is the supreme Author of our action, abstractedly taken, but our own vitiosity is the cause of our acting amiss.

I shall conclude this article with two or three observations, and—

(1) I would infer that, if we would maintain the doctrine of God's omnipotence, we must insist upon that of His universal agency; the latter cannot be denied without giving up the former. Disprove that He is almighty, and then we will grant that His influence and

operations are limited and circumscribed. Luther* says, "God would not be a respectable Being if He were not almighty, and the doer of all things that are done, or if anything could come to pass in which He had no hand." God has, at least, a physical influence on whatsoever is done by His creatures, whether trivial or important, good or evil. Judas as truly lived, moved and had his being from God as Peter, and Satan himself as much as Gabriel, for to say that sin exempts the sinner from the Divine government and jurisdiction is abridging the power of God with a witness, nay, is rasing it from its very foundations.

(2) This doctrine of God's omnipotence has a native tendency to awaken in our hearts that reverence for and fear of the Divine Majesty, which none can either receive or retain, but those who believe Him to be infinitely powerful, and to work all things after the counsel of His own will. This godly fear is a sovereign antidote against sin, for, if I really believe that God, by His unintermitted operation upon my soul, produces actions in me, which, being simply good, receive their malignancy from the corruption of my nature (and even those works that stand opposed to sins are, more or less, infected with this moral leprosy), and if I consider that, should I yield myself a slave to actual iniquity, God can, and justly might, as He has frequently done by others, give me up to a reprobate mind and punish one sin by leaving me to the commission of another, surely such reflections as these must fill me with awful apprehensions of the Divine purity, power and greatness, and make me watch continually as well against the inward risings as the outward appearance of evil.

(3) This doctrine is also useful, as it tends to inspire us with true humility of soul, and to lay us, as impotent dust and ashes, at the feet of sovereign Omnipotence. It teaches us, what too many are fatally ignorant of, the

---

* De Serv. Arb. c. 160.

blessed lesson of *self-despair*, *i.e.*, that, in a state of unregeneracy, our wisdom is folly, our strength weakness and our righteousness nothing worth; that therefore we can do nothing, either to the glory of God or the spiritual benefit of ourselves and others, but through the ability which He giveth; that in him our strength lieth, and from Him all our help must come. Supposing we believe that whatsoever is done below or above, God doeth it Himself; that all things depend both as to their being and operation upon His omnipotent arm and mighty support; that we cannot even sin, much less do any good thing, if He withdrew His aid; and that all men are in His hand, as clay in the hand of the potter—I say, did we really believe all these points and see them in the light of the Divine Spirit, how can it be reasonably supposed that we could wax insolent against this great God, behave contemptuously and superciliously in the world, or boast of anything we have or do? Luther* informs us that "he used frequently to be much offended at this doctrine, because it drove him to *self-despair*, but that he afterwards found that this sort of despair was salutary and profitable, and near akin to Divine grace."

(4) We are hereby taught not only humility before God, but likewise dependence on Him and resignation to Him. For if we are thoroughly persuaded that of ourselves and in our own strength we cannot either do good or evil, but that, being originally created by God, we are incessantly supported, moved, influenced and directed by Him, this way or that, as He pleases, the natural inference from hence will be that with simple faith we cast ourselves entirely as on the bosom of His providence; commit all our care and solicitude to His hand; praying, without hesitation or reserve, that His will may be done in us, on us, and by us; and that, in all His dealing with us, He may consult His own glory alone. This holy passiveness is the very apex of Christianity. All

---

* De Serv. Arb. c. 161.

the desires of our great Redeemer Himself were reducible
to these two : that the will of God might be done, and
that the glory of God might be displayed. These were
the highest and supreme marks at which He aimed
throughout the whole course of His spotless life and in-
conceivably tremendous sufferings. Happy, thrice happy
that man who hath thus far attained the mind that was
in Christ.

(5) The comfortable belief of this doctrine has a
tendency to excite and keep alive within us that fortitude
which is so ornamental to, and necessary for us while we
abide in this wilderness. For if I believe, with the
apostle, that " all things are of God " (2 Cor. v. 18), I
shall be less liable to perturbation when afflicted, and
learn more easily to possess my soul in patience. This
was Job's support ; he was not overcome with rage and
despair when he received news that the Sabeans had
carried off his cattle and slain his servants, and that the
remainder of both were consumed with fire ; that the
Chaldeans had robbed him of his camels, and that his
seven sons were crushed to death by the falling of the
house where they were sitting : he resolved all these
misfortunes into the agency of God, His power and
sovereignty, and even thanked Him for doing what He
would with His own (Job i. 21). If another should
slander me in word, or injure me in deed, I shall not be
prone to anger, when, with David, I consider that the
Lord hath bidden him (2 Sam. xvi. 10).

(6) This should stir us up to fervent and incessant
prayer. For, does God work powerfully and benignly
in the hearts of His elect? and is He the sole cause of
every action they do, which is truly and spiritually good?
Then it should be our prayer that He would work in us
likewise both to will and to do of His good pleasure, and
if, on self-examination, we find reason to trust that some
good thing is wrought in us, it should put us upon thankfulness unfeigned, and cause us to glory, not in ourselves,
but in Him. On the other hand, does God manifest His

displeasure against the wicked by blinding, hardening
and giving them up to perpetrate iniquity with greedi-
ness? which judicial acts of God are both a punishment
for their sin and also eventual additions to it, we should
be the more incited to deprecate these tremendous evils,
and to beseech the King of heaven that He would not
thus "lead us into temptation." So much concerning
the omnipotence of God.

THE JUSTICE OF GOD.

V.—I shall now take notice of HIS JUSTICE.

POSITION 1.—God is infinitely, absolutely and unchangeably just.

The justice of God may be considered either imma-
nently, as it is in Himself, which is, properly speaking,
the same with His holiness; or transiently and relatively,
as it respects His right conduct towards His creatures,
which is properly justice. By the former He is all that
is holy, just and good; by the latter, He is manifested
to be so in all His dealings with angels and men. For
the first, see Deut. xxxii. 4; Psa. xcii. 15; for the second,
Job viii. 3; Psa. cxlv. 17. Hence it follows that whatever God either wills or does, however it may, at first
sight, seem to clash with our ideas of right and wrong,
cannot really be unjust. It is certain that for a season He
sorely afflicted His righteous servant Job, and, on the
other hand, enriched the Sabeans, an infidel and lawless
nation, with a profusion of wealth and a series of success;
before Jacob and Esau were born, or had done either
good or evil, He loved and chose the former and reprobated the latter; He gave repentance to Peter and left
Judas to perish in his sin; and as in all ages, so to this
day, "He hath mercy on whom He will, and whom He
will He hardeneth." In all which He acts most justly
and righteously, and there is no iniquity with Him.

POSITION 2.—The Deity may be considered in a threefold view : as God of all, as Lord of all, and as Judge
of all.

(1) As God of all, He created, sustains and exhilarates the whole universe; causes His sun to shine, and His rain to fall upon the evil and the good (Matt. v.), and is σωτηρ πάντων ανθρώπων, the Preserver of all men (1 Tim. iv. 10). For as He is infinitely and supremely good, so also is He communicative of His goodness, as appears not only from His creation of all things, but especially from His providential benignity. Everything has its being from Him as Creator, and its well-being from Him as a bountiful Preserver.

(2) As Lord or Sovereign of all, He does as He will (and has a most unquestionable right to do so) with His own, and in particular fixes and determines the everlasting state of every individual person, as He sees fit. It is essential to absolute sovereignty that the sovereign have it in his power to dispose of those over whom his jurisdiction extends, just as he pleases, without being accountable to any; and God, whose authority is unbounded, none being exempt from it, may, with the strictest holiness and justice, love or hate, elect or reprobate, save or destroy any of His creatures, whether human or angelic, according to His own free pleasure and sovereign purpose.

(3) As Judge of all, He ratifies what He does as Lord by rendering to all according to their works, by punishing the wicked, and rewarding those whom it was His will to esteem righteous and to make holy.

POSITION 3.—Whatever things God wills or does are not willed and done by Him because they were in their own nature and previously to His willing them, just and right, or because, from their intrinsic fitness, He ought to will and do them; but they are therefore just, right and proper because He, who is holiness itself, wills and does them.

Hence, Abraham looked upon it as a righteous action to slay his innocent son. Why did he so esteem it, because the law of God authorised murder? No; for, on the contrary, both the law of God and the law of nature peremptorily forbade it; but the holy patriarch well knew that the will of God is the only rule of justice, and that what He pleases to command is, on that very account, just and righteous.*

POSITION 4.—It follows that, although our works are to be examined by the revealed will of God, and be denominated materially good or evil, as they agree or disagree with it, yet the works of God Himself cannot be brought to any test whatever, for, His will being the grand universal law, He Himself cannot be, properly speaking, subject to or obliged by any law superior to that. Many things are done by Him, such as choosing and reprobating men, without any respect had to their works; suffering people to fall into sin, when, if it so pleased Him, He might prevent it; leaving many backsliding professors to go on and perish in their apostacy, when it is in His Divine power to sanctify and set them right; drawing some by His grace, and permitting many others to continue in sin and unregeneracy; condemning those to future misery whom, if He pleased, He could undoubtedly save; with innumerable instances of the like nature (which might be mentioned), and which, if done by us, would be apparently unjust, inasmuch as they would not square with the revealed will of God, which is the great and only safe rule of our practice. But when *He* does these and such like things, they cannot but be holy, equitable and worthy of Himself; for, since His will is essentially and unchangeably just, whatever He does, in consequence of that will, must be just and good likewise. From what has been delivered under this fifth head, I would infer that they who deny the power God has of doing as He will with His creatures, and exclaim against unconditional decrees as cruel, tyrannical and unjust, either know not what they say nor whereof they affirm, or are wilful blasphemers of His name and perverse rebels against His sovereignty, to which, at last, however unwillingly, they will be forced to submit.

---

* Compare also Exod. iii. 22 with Exod. xx. 15.

THE MERCY OF GOD.

VI.—I shall conclude this introduction with briefly considering, in the sixth and last place, THE MERCY OF GOD.

POSITION 1.—The Deity is, throughout the Scriptures, represented as infinitely gracious and merciful (Exod. xxxiv. 6; Nehem. ix. 17; Psalm ciii. 8; 1 Peter i. 3).

When we call the Divine mercy infinite, we do not mean that it is, in a way of grace, extended to all men without exception (and supposing it was, even then it would be very improperly denominated infinite on that account, since the objects of it, though all men taken together, would not amount to a multitude strictly and properly infinite), but that His mercy towards His own elect, as it knew no beginning, so is it infinite in duration, and shall know neither period nor intermission.

POSITION 2.—Mercy is not in the Deity, as it is in us, a passion or affection, everything of that kind being incompatible with the purity, perfection, independency and unchangeableness of His nature; but when this attribute is predicated of Him, it only notes His free and eternal will or purpose of making some of the fallen race happy by delivering them from the guilt and dominion of sin, and communicating Himself to them in a way consistent with His own inviolable justice, truth and holiness. This seems to be the proper definition of mercy as it relates to the spiritual and eternal good of those who are its objects.

POSITION 3.—But it should be observed that the mercy of God, taken in its more large and indefinite sense, may be considered (1) as general and (2) as special. His general mercy is no other than what we commonly call His bounty, by which He is, more or less, providentially good to all mankind, both elect and non-elect (Matt. v. 45; Luke vi. 35; Acts xiv. 17, xvii. 25, 28). By His special mercy He, as Lord of all, hath, in a spiritual sense, compassion on as many of the fallen race as are the objects of His free and eternal favour, the effects of which special mercy are the redemption and justification of their persons through the satisfaction of Christ, the effectual vocation, regeneration and sanctification of them by His Spirit, the infallible and final preservation of them in a state of grace on earth, and their everlasting glorification in heaven.

POSITION 4.—There is no contradiction, whether real or seeming, between these two assertions : (1) that the blessings of grace and glory are peculiar to those whom God hath, in His decree of predestination, set apart for Himself, and (2) that the Gospel declaration runs, that whosoever willeth may take of the water of life freely (Rev. xxii. 17). Since, in the first place, none can will, or unfeignedly and spiritually desire, a part in these privileges but those whom God previously makes willing and desirous ; and, secondly, that He gives this will to, and excites this desire in, none but His own elect.

POSITION 5.—Since ungodly men, who are totally and finally destitute of Divine grace, cannot know what this mercy is, nor form any proper apprehensions of it, much less by faith embrace and rely upon it for themselves, and since daily experience, as well as the Scriptures of truth, teaches us that God doth not open the eyes of the reprobate as He doth the eyes of His elect, nor savingly enlighten their understandings, it evidently follows that His mercy was never, from the very first, designed for them, neither will it be applied to them ; but, both in designation and application, is proper and peculiar to those only who are predestinated to life, as it is written, " the election hath obtained, and the rest were blinded " (Rom xi. 7).

POSITION 6.—The whole work of salvation, together with everything that is in order to it or stands in connection with it, is sometimes, in Scripture, comprised under the single term mercy, to show that mere love and absolute grace were the grand cause why the elect are saved, and that all merit, worthiness and good qualifications of theirs were entirely excluded from having any influence on the Divine will why they should be chosen, redeemed and glorified above others. When it is said, " He hath mercy on whom He will have mercy " (Rom. ix.), it is as much as if the apostle had said, " God elected, ransomed, justified, regenerates, sanctifies and glorifies whom He pleases," every one of these great privileges being briefly summed up and virtually included in that comprehensive phrase, " He hath mercy."

POSITION 7.—It follows that, whatever favour is bestowed on us, whatever good thing is in us or wrought by us, whether in will, word or deed, and whatever blessings else we receive from God, from election quite home to glorification, all proceed, merely and entirely, from the good pleasure of His will and His mercy towards us in Christ Jesus. To Him therefore the praise is due, who putteth the difference between man and man by having compassion on some and not on others.

THE DOCTRINE OF
ABSOLUTE PREDESTINATION
STATED AND ASSERTED.

CHAPTER I.

WHEREIN THE TERMS COMMONLY MADE USE OF IN TREATING OF THIS SUBJECT ARE DEFINED AND EXPLAINED.

HAVING considered the attributes of God as laid down in Scripture, and so far cleared our way to the doctrine of predestination, I shall, before I enter further on the subject, explain the principal terms generally made use of when treating of it, and settle their true meaning. In discoursing on the Divine decrees, mention is frequently made of God's love and hatred, of election and reprobation, and of the Divine purpose, foreknowledge and predestination, each of which we shall distinctly and briefly consider.

I.—When love is predicated of God, we do not mean that He is possessed of it as a passion or affection. In us it is such, but if, considered in that sense, it should be ascribed to the Deity, it would be utterly subversive of the simplicity, perfection and independency of His being. Love, therefore, when attributed to Him, signifies—

(1) His eternal benevolence, *i.e.*, His everlasting will, purpose and determination to deliver, bless and save His people. Of this, no good works wrought by them are in any sense the cause. Neither are even the merits of Christ Himself to be considered as any way moving or exciting this good will of God to His elect, since the gift of Christ, to be their Mediator and Redeemer, is itself an effect of this free and eternal favour borne to them by God the Father (John iii. 16). His love towards them arises merely from " the good pleasure of His own will,"

without the least regard to anything *ad extra* or out of Himself.

(2) The term implies complacency, delight and approbation. With this love God cannot love even His elect as considered in themselves, because in that view they are guilty, polluted sinners, but they were, from all eternity, objects of it, as they stood united to Christ and partakers of His righteousness.

(3) Love implies actual beneficence, which, properly speaking, is nothing else than the effect or accomplishment of the other two : those are the cause of this. This actual beneficence respects all blessings, whether of a temporal, spiritual or eternal nature. Temporal good things are indeed indiscriminately bestowed in a greater or less degree on all, whether elect or reprobate, but they are given in a covenant way and as blessings to the elect only, to whom also the other benefits respecting grace and glory are peculiar. And this love of beneficence, no less than that of benevolence and complacency, is absolutely free, and irrespective of any worthiness in man.

II.—When hatred is ascribed to God, it implies (1) a negation of benevolence, or a resolution not to have mercy on such and such men, nor to endue them with any of those graces which stand connected with eternal life. So, " Esau have I hated " (Rom. ix.), *i.e.*, " I did, from all eternity, determine within Myself not to have mercy on him." The sole cause of which awful negation is not merely the unworthiness of the persons hated, but the sovereignty and freedom of the Divine will. (2) It denotes displeasure and dislike, for sinners who are not interested in Christ cannot but be infinitely displeasing to and loathsome in the sight of eternal purity. (3) It signifies a positive will to punish and destroy the reprobate for their sins, of which will, the infliction of misery upon them hereafter, is but the necessary effect and actual execution.

III.—The term election, that so very frequently occurs in Scripture, is there taken in a fourfold sense, and most

commonly signifies (1) "That eternal, sovereign, unconditional, particular and immutable act of God where He
selected some from among all mankind and of every
nation under heaven to be redeemed and everlastingly
saved by Christ."

(2) It sometimes and more rarely signifies "that
gracious and almighty act of the Divine Spirit, whereby
God actually and visibly separates His elect from the
world by effectual calling." This is nothing but the
manifestation and partial fulfilment of the former election, and by it the objects of predestinating grace are
sensibly led into the communion of saints, and visibly
added to the number of God's declared professing people.
Of this our Lord makes mention : "Because I have
chosen you out of the world, therefore the world hateth
you " (John xv. 19). Where it should seem the choice
spoken of does not refer so much to God's eternal, immanent act of election as His open manifest one, whereby
He powerfully and efficaciously called the disciples forth
from the world of the unconverted, and quickened them
from above in conversion.

(3) By election is sometimes meant, "God's taking
a whole nation, community or body of men into external
covenant with Himself by giving them the advantage of
revelation, or His written word, as the rule of their belief
and practice, when other nations are without it." In
this sense the whole body of the Jewish nation was indiscriminately called elect, because that " unto them were
committed the oracles of God " (Deut. vii. 6). Now all
that are thus elected are not therefore necessarily saved,
but many of them may be, and are, reprobates, as those
of whom our Lord says (Matt. xiii. 20), that they "hear
the word, and anon with joy receive it," etc. And the
apostle says, "They went out from us " (*i.e.*, being
favoured with the same Gospel revelation we were, they
professed themselves true believers, no less than we),
" but they were not of us " (*i.e.*, they were not, with us,
chosen of God unto everlasting life, nor did they ever in

reality possess that faith of His operation which He gave to us, for if they had in this sense "been of us, they would, no doubt, have continued with us" (1 John ii. 19), they would have manifested the sincerity of their professions and the truth of their conversion by enduring to the end and being saved. And even this external revelation, though it is not necessarily connected with eternal happiness, is nevertheless productive of very many and great advantages to the people and places where it is vouchsafed, and is made known to some nations and kept back* from others, "according to the good pleasure of Him who worketh all things after the counsel of His own will."

(4) And, lastly, election sometimes signifies "the temporary designation of some person or persons to the filling up some particular station in the visible church or office in civil life." So Judas was chosen to the apostleship (John vi. 70), and Saul to be the king of Israel (1 Sam. x. 24). Thus much for the use of the word election.

IV.—On the contrary, reprobation denotes either (1) God's eternal preterition of some men, when He chose others to glory, and His predestination of them to fill up the measure of their iniquities and then to receive the just punishment of their crimes, even "destruction from the presence of the Lord, and from the glory of His power." This is the primary, most obvious and most frequent sense in which the word is used. It may likewise signify (2) God's forbearing to call by His grace those whom He hath thus ordained to condemnation, but this is only a temporary preterition, and a consequence of that which was from eternity. (3) And, lastly, the word may be taken in another sense as denoting God's refusal to grant to some nations the light of the Gospel revelation. This may be considered as a kind of national reprobation, which yet does not imply that every indivi-

---

* See Psalm cxlvii. 19, 20.

dual person who lives in such a country must therefore unavoidably perish for ever, any more than that every individual who lives in a land called Christian is therefore in a state of salvation. There are, no doubt, elect persons among the former as well as reprobate ones among the latter. By a very little attention to the context any reader may easily discover in which of these several senses the words elect and reprobate are used whenever they occur in Scripture.

V.—Mention is frequently made in Scripture of the purpose* of God, which is no other than His gracious intention from eternity of making His elect everlastingly happy in Christ.

VI.—When foreknowledge is ascribed to God, the word imports (1) that general prescience whereby He knew from all eternity both what He Himself would do, and what His creatures, in consequence of His efficacious and permissive decree, should do likewise. The Divine foreknowledge, considered in this view, is absolutely universal; it extends to all beings that did, do or ever

---

* The *purpose* of God does not seem to differ at all from *predestination*, that being, as well as this, an eternal, free and unchangeable act of His will. Besides, the word " purpose," when predicated of God in the New Testament, always denotes His design of saving His elect, and that only (Rom. viii. 28, ix. 11; Eph. i. 11, iii. 11; 2 Tim. i. 9). As does the term " predestination," which throughout the whole New Testament never signifies the appointment of the non-elect to wrath, but singly and solely the fore-appointment of the elect to grace and glory, though, in common theological writings, predestination is spoken of as extending to whatever God does, both in a way of permission and efficiency, as, in the utmost sense of the term, it does. It is worthy of the reader's notice that the original word, προθεσις which we render purpose, signifies not only an appointment, but a fore-appointment, and such a fore-appointment as is efficacious and cannot be obstructed, but shall most assuredly issue in a full accomplishment, which gave occasion to the following judicious remark of a late learned writer : " προθεσις *a Paulo sæpe usurpatur in electionis negotio, ad designandum consilium hoc Dei non esse inanem quandam et inefficacem velleitatem ; sed constans, determinatum, et immutabile Dei propositum. Vox enim est efficaciæ summæ, ut notant grammatici veteres ; et signate vocatur a Paulo,* προθεσις του τα παντα ενεργγευτος *consilium illius, qui efficaciter omnia operatur ex beneplacito suo.*"—Turretin. Institut. Tom. 1, loc. 4, quæst. 7. s. 12.

shall exist, and to all actions that ever have been, that are or shall be done, whether good or evil, natural, civil or moral. (2) The word often denotes that special prescience which has for its objects His own elect, and them alone, whom He is in a peculiar sense said to know and foreknow (Psa. i. 6; John x. 27; 2 Tim. ii. 19; Rom. viii. 29; 1 Peter i. 2), and this knowledge is connected with, or rather the *same* with love, favour and approbation.

VII.—We come now to consider the meaning of the word predestination, and how it is taken in Scripture. The verb predestinate is of Latin original, and signifies, in that tongue, to deliberate beforehand with one's self how one shall act; and in consequence of such deliberation to constitute, fore-ordain and predetermine where, when, how and by whom anything shall be done, and to what end it shall be done. So the Greek verb, Προορίζω, which exactly answers to the English word predestinate, and is rendered by it, signifies to resolve beforehand within one's self what to do; and, before the thing resolved on is actually effected, to appoint it to some certain use, and direct it to some determinate end. The Hebrew verb Habhdel has likewise much the same signification.

Now, none but wise men are capable (especially in matters of great importance) of rightly determining what to do, and how to accomplish a proper end by just, suitable and effectual means; and if this is, confessedly, a very material part of true wisdom, who so fit to dispose of men and assign each individual his sphere of action in this world, and his place in the world to come, as the all-wise God? And yet, alas! how many are there who cavil at those eternal decrees which, were we capable of fully and clearly understanding them, would appear to be as just as they are sovereign and as wise as they are incomprehensible! Divine preordination has for its objects all things that are created : no creature, whether rational or irrational, animate or inanimate, is exempted from its influence. All beings whatever, from the highest angel to the meanest reptile, and from the meanest reptile to the minutest atom, are the objects of God's eternal decrees and particular providence. However, the ancient fathers only make use of the word predestination as it refers to angels or men, whether good or evil, and it is used by the apostle Paul in a more limited sense still, so as, by it, to mean only that branch of it which respects God's election and designation of His people to eternal life (Rom. viii. 30; Eph. i. 11).

But, that we may more justly apprehend the import of this word, and the ideas intended to be conveyed by it, it may be proper to observe that the term predestination. theologically taken, admits of a fourfold definition, and may be considered as (1) '' that eternal, most wise and immutable decree of God, whereby He did from before all time determine and ordain to create, dispose of and direct to some particular end every person and thing to which He has given, or is yet to give, being, and to make the whole creation subservient to and declarative of His own glory.'' Of this decree actual providence is the execution. (2) Predestination may be considered as relating generally to mankind, and them only; and in this view we define it to be '' the everlasting, sovereign and invariable purpose of God, whereby He did determine within Himself to create Adam in His own image and likeness, and then to permit his fall; and to suffer him thereby to plunge himself and his whole posterity '' (inasmuch as they all sinned in him, not only virtually, but also federally and representatively) '' into the dreadful abyss of sin, misery and death.'' (3) Consider predestination as relating to the elect only, and it is '' that eternal, unconditional, particular and irreversible act of the Divine will whereby, in matchless love and adorable sovereignty, God determined with Himself to deliver a certain number of Adam's degenerate* offspring out of

---

* When we say that the decree of predestination to life and death respects man as fallen, we do not mean that the fall was actually antecedent to that decree, for the decree is truly and properly eternal.

that sinful and miserable estate into which, by his primitive transgression, they were to fall," and in which sad condition they were equally involved, with those who were not chosen, but, being pitched upon and singled out by God the Father to be vessels of grace and salvation (not for anything in them that could recommend them to His favour or entitle them to His notice, but merely because He would show Himself gracious to them), they were, in time, actually redeemed by Christ, are effectually called by His Spirit, justified, adopted, sanctified, and preserved safe to His heavenly kingdom. The supreme end of this decree is the manifestation of His own infinitely glorious and amiably tremendous perfections; the inferior or subordinate end is the happiness and salvation of them who are thus freely elected. (4) Predestination, as it regards the reprobate, is " that eternal, most holy, sovereign and immutable act of God's will, whereby He hath determined to leave some men to perish in their sins, and to be justly punished for them."

---

as all God's immanent acts undoubtedly are, whereas the fall took place in time. What we intend, then, is only this, viz., that God (for reasons, without doubt, worthy of Himself, and of which we are by no means in this life competent judges), having, from everlasting, peremptorily ordained to suffer the fall of Adam, did likewise, from everlasting, consider the human race as fallen; and out of the whole mass of mankind, thus viewed and foreknown as impure and obnoxious to condemnation, vouchsafed to select some particular persons (who collectively make up a very great though percisely determinate number) in and on whom He would make known the ineffable riches of His mercy.

CHAPTER II.

WHEREIN THE DOCTRINE OF PREDESTINATION IS EXPLAINED AS IT RELATES IN GENERAL TO ALL MEN.

THUS much being premised with relation to the Scripture terms commonly made use of in this controversy, we shall now proceed to take a nearer view of this high and mysterious article, and—

I.—We, with the Scriptures, assert that there is a predestination of some particular persons to life for the praise of the glory of Divine grace, and a predestination of other particular persons to death, which death of punishment they shall inevitably undergo, and that justly, on account of their sins.

(1) There is a predestination of some particular persons to life, so " Many are called, but few chosen " (Matt. xx. 15), *i.e.*, the Gospel revelation comes, indiscriminately, to great multitudes, but few, comparatively speaking, are spiritually and eternally the better for it, and these few, to whom it is the savour of life unto life, are therefore savingly benefited by it, because they are the chosen or elect of God. To the same effect are the following passages, among many others : "For the elect's sake, those days shall be shortened " (Matt. xxiv. 22). "As many as were ordained to eternal life, believed " (Acts xiii. 48). "Whom He did predestinate, them He also called " (Rom. viii. 30), and ver. 33, " Who shall lay anything to the charge of God's elect? " "According as He hath chosen us in Him, before the foundation of the world, that we should be holy . . . Having predestinated us to the adoption of children, by Jesus Christ, unto Himself, according to the good pleasure of His will" (Eph. i. 4, 5). "Who hath saved us, and called us with an holy calling, not according to our works, but according to His own purpose and grace which was given us, in Christ, before the world began " (2 Tim. i. 9).

(2) This election of certain individuals unto eternal life was for the praise of the glory of Divine grace. This is expressly asserted, in so many words, by the apostle (Eph. i. 5, 6). Grace, or mere favour, was the impulsive cause of all : it was the main spring, which set all the inferior wheels in motion. It was an act of grace in God to choose any, when He might have passed by all. It was an act of sovereign grace to choose this man rather than that, when both were equally undone in themselves, and alike obnoxious to His displeasure. In a word, since election is not of works, and does not proceed on the least regard had to any worthiness in its objects, it must be of free, unbiassed grace, but election is not of works (Rom. xi. 5, 6), therefore it is solely of grace.

(3) There is, on the other hand, a predestination of some particular persons to death. "If our Gospel be hid, it is hid to them that are lost" (2 Cor. iv. 3). "Who stumble at the word being disobedient; whereunto also they were appointed" (1 Pet. ii. 8). "These as natural brute beasts, made to be taken and destroyed" (2 Pet. ii. 12). "There are certain men, crept in unawares, who were before, of old, ordained to this condemnation" (Jude 4). "Whose names were not written in the book of life from the foundation of the world" (Rev. xvii. 8). But of this we shall treat professedly, and more at large, in the fifth chapter.

(4) This future death they shall inevitably undergo, for, as God will certainly save all whom He wills should be saved, so He will as surely condemn all whom He wills shall be condemned; for He is the Judge of the whole earth, whose decree shall stand, and from whose sentence there is no appeal. "Hath He said, and shall He not make it good? hath He spoken, and shall it not come to pass?" And His decree is this : that these (i.e., the non-elect, who are left under the guilt of final impenitence, unbelief and sin) "shall go away into everlasting punishment, and the righteous (i.e., those who, in consequence of their election in Christ and union to

Him, are justly reputed and really constituted such) shall enter into life eternal " (Matt. xxv. 46).

(5) The reprobate shall undergo this punishment justly and on account of their sins.   Sin is the meritorious and immediate cause of any man's damnation.   God condemns and punishes the non-elect, not merely as men, but as sinners, and had it pleased the great Governor of the universe to have entirely prevented sin from having any entrance into the world, it would seem as if He could not, consistently with His known attributes, have condemned any man at all.   But, as all sin is properly meritorious of eternal death, and all men are sinners, they who are condemned are condemned most justly, and those who are saved are saved in a way of sovereign mercy through the vicarious obedience and death of Christ for them.

Now this twofold predestination, of some to life and of others to death (if it may be called twofold, both being constituent parts of the same decree), cannot be denied without likewise denying (1) most express and frequent declarations of Scripture, and (2) the very existence of God, for, since God is a Being perfectly simple, free from all accident and composition, and yet a will to save some and punish others is very often predicated of Him in Scripture, and an immovable decree to do this, in consequence of His will, is likewise ascribed to Him, and a perfect foreknowledge of the sure and certain accomplishment of what He has thus willed and decreed is also attributed to Him, it follows that whoever denies this will, decree and foreknowledge of God, does implicitly and virtually deny God Himself, since His will, decree and foreknowledge are no other than God Himself willing and decreeing and foreknowing.

II.—We assert that God did from eternity decree to make man in His own image, and also decreed to suffer him to fall from that image in which he should be created, and thereby to forfeit the happiness with which he was invested, which decree and the consequences of it were not limited to Adam only, but included and extended to all his natural posterity.

Something of this was hinted already in the preceding chapter, and we shall now proceed to the proof of it.

(1) That God did make man in His own image is evident from Scripture (Gen. i. 27).

(2) That He decreed from eternity so to make man is as evident, since for God to do anything without having decreed it, or fixed a previous plan in His own mind, would be a manifest imputation on His wisdom, and if He decreed that now, or at any time, which He did not always decree, He could not be unchangeable.

(3) That man actually did fall from the Divine image and his original happiness is the undoubted voice of Scripture (Gen. iii.), and

(4) That he fell in consequence of the Divine decree* we prove thus : God was either willing that Adam should fall, or unwilling, or indifferent about it. If God was unwilling that Adam should transgress, how came it to pass that he did? Is man stronger and is Satan wiser than He that made them? Surely no. Again, could not God, had it so pleased Him, have hindered the tempter's access to paradise? or have created man, as He did the elect angels, with a will invariably determined to good only and incapable of being biassed to evil? or, at least, have made the grace and strength, with which He endued Adam, actually effectual to the resisting of all solicitations to sin? None but atheists would answer these questions in the negative. Surely, if God had not willed the fall, He could, and no doubt would, have prevented it ; but He did not prevent it : ergo, He willed it. And if He willed it, He certainly decreed it, for the decree of God is nothing else but the seal and ratification of His will. He does nothing but what He decreed, and He decreed nothing which He did not will, and both will and

---

* See this article judiciously stated and nervously asserted by Witsius in his Œcon. l. 1, cap. 8, s. 10-25.

decree are absolutely eternal, though the execution of both be in time. The only way to evade the force of this reasoning is to say that "God was indifferent and unconcerned whether man stood or fell." But in what a shameful, unworthy light does this represent the Deity! Is it possible for us to imagine that God could be an idle, careless spectator of one of the most important events that ever came to pass? Are not "the very hairs of our head all numbered"? or does "a sparrow fall to the ground without our heavenly Father"? If, then, things the most trivial and worthless are subject to the appointment of His decree and the control of His providence, how much more is *man*, the masterpiece of this lower creation? and above all *that* man Adam, who when recent from his Maker's hands was the living image of God Himself, and very little inferior to angels! and on whose perseverance was suspended the welfare not of himself only, but likewise that of the whole world. But, so far was God from being indifferent in this matter, that there is nothing whatever about which He is so, for He worketh all things, without exception, "after the counsel of His own will" (Eph. i. 11), consequently, if He positively wills whatever is done, He cannot be indifferent with regard to anything. On the whole, if God was not unwilling that Adam should fall, He must have been willing that he should, since between God's willing and nilling there is no medium. And is it not highly rational as well as Scriptural, nay, is it not absolutely necessary to suppose that the fall was not contrary to the will and determination of God? since, if it was, His will (which the apostle represents as being irresistible, Rom. ix. 19) was apparently frustrated and His determination rendered of worse than none effect. And how dishonourable to, how inconsistent with, and how notoriously subversive of the dignity of God such a blasphemous supposition would be, and how irreconcileable with every one of His allowed attributes is very easy to observe.

(5) That man by his fall forfeited the happiness with

which he was invested is evident as well from Scripture
as from experience (Gen. iii. 7-24; Rom. v. 12; Gal.
iii. 10). He first sinned (and the essence of sin lies in
disobedience to the command of God) and then immediately became miserable, misery being through the Divine
appointment, the natural and inseparable concomitant
of sin.

(6) That the fall and its sad consequences did not
terminate solely in Adam, but affected his whole posterity, is the doctrine of the sacred oracles (Psalm li. 5;
Rom. v. 12-19; 1 Cor. xv. 22; Eph. ii. 3). Besides, not
only spiritual and eternal, but likewise temporal death is
the wages of sin (Rom. vi. 23; James i. 15), and yet we
see that millions of infants, who never in their own
persons either did or could commit sin, die continually.
It follows that either God must be unjust in punishing
the innocent, or that these infants are some way or the
other guilty creatures; if they are not so in themselves
(I mean actually so by their own commission of sin),
they must be so in some other person, and who that
person is let Scripture say (Rom. v. 12, 18; 1 Cor. xv. 22).
And, I ask, how can these be with equity sharers in
Adam's punishment unless they are chargeable with his
sin? and how can they be fairly chargeable with his sin
unless he was their federal head and representative, and
acted in their name, and sustained their persons, when
he fell?

III.—We assert that as all men universally are not
elected to salvation, so neither are all men universally
ordained to condemnation. This follows from what has
been proved already; however, I shall subjoin some
further demonstration of these two positions.

(1) All men universally are not elected to salvation,
and, first, this may be evinced *a posteriori;* it is undeniable from Scripture that God will not in the last day
save every individual of mankind! (Dan. xii. 2; Matt.
xxv. 46; John v. 29). Therefore, say we, God never
designed to save every individual, since, if He had, every

individual would and must be saved, for "His counsel shall stand, and He will do all His pleasure." (See what we have already advanced on this head in the first chapter under the second article, Position 8). Secondly, this may be evinced also from God's foreknowledge. The Deity from all eternity, and consequently at the very time He gives life and being to a reprobate, certainly foreknew, and knows, in consequence of His own decree, that such a one would fall short of salvation. Now, if God foreknew this, He must have predetermined it, because His own will is the foundation of His decrees, and His decrees are the foundation of His prescience; He therefore foreknowing futurities, because by His predestination He hath rendered their futurition certain and inevitable. Neither is it possible, in the very nature of the thing, that they should be elected to salvation, or ever obtain it, whom God foreknew should perish, for then the Divine act of preterition would be changeable, wavering and precarious, the Divine foreknowledge would be deceived, and the Divine will impeded. All which are utterly impossible. Lastly, that all men are not chosen to life, nor created to that end is evident in that there are some who were hated of God before they were born (Rom. ix. 11-13), are "fitted for destruction" (ver. 22), and " made for the day of evil " (Prov. xvi. 1).

But (2) all men universally are not ordained to condemnation. There are some who are chosen (Matt. xx. 16). An election, or elect number, who obtain grace and salvation, while "the rest are blinded " (Rom. xi. 7), a little flock, to whom it is the Father's good pleasure to give the kingdom (Luke xii. 32). A people whom the Lord hath reserved (Jer. l. 20) and formed for Himself (Isa. xliii. 21). A peculiarly favoured race, to whom " it is given to know the mysteries of the kingdom of heaven," while to others "it is not given" (Matt. xiii. 11), " a remnant according to the election of grace " (Rom. xi. 5), whom " God hath not appointed to wrath, but to obtain salvation by Jesus Christ " (1 Thes. v. 9). In a word, who are " a chosen generation, a royal priesthood, a holy nation, a peculiar people, that they should show forth the praises of Him who hath called them out of darkness into His marvellous light " (1 Peter ii. 9), and whose names for that very end " are in the book of life " (Phil. iv. 3) and written in heaven (Luke x. 20 ; Heb. xii. 23). Luther* observes that in Rom. ix., x. and xi. the apostle particularly insists on the doctrine of pre-destination, " Because," says he, " all things whatever arise from and depend upon the Divine appointment, whereby it was preordained who should receive the word of life and who should disbelieve it, who should be delivered from their sins and who should be hardened in them, who should be justified and who condemned."

IV.—We assert that the number of the elect, and also of the reprobate, is so fixed and determinate that neither can be augmented or diminished. It is written of God that " He telleth the number of the stars, and calleth them all by their names " (Psalm cxlvii. 4). Now, it is as incompatible with the infinite wisdom and know-ledge of the all-comprehending God to be ignorant of the names and number of the rational creatures He has made as that He should be ignorant of the stars and the other inanimate products of His almighty power, and if He knows all men in general, taken in the lump, He may well be said, in a more near and special sense, to know them that are His by election (2 Tim. ii. 19). And if He knows who are His, He must, consequently, know who are not His, *i.e.*, whom and how many He hath left in the corrupt mass to be justly punished for their sins. Grant this (and who can help granting a truth so self-evident?), and it follows that the number, as well of the elect as of the reprobate, is fixed and certain, otherwise God would be said to know that which is not true, and His knowledge must be false and delusive, and so no knowledge at all, since that which is, in itself, at best,

---

* *In Præfat, ad Epist. ad Rom.*

but precarious, can never be the foundation of sure and infallible knowledge. But that God does indeed precisely know, to a man, who are, and are not the objects of His electing favour is evident from such Scriptures as these : " Thou hast found grace in My sight, and I know thee by name " (Exod. xxxiii. 17). " Before I formed thee in the belly, I knew thee " (Jer. i. 5). " Your names are written in heaven " (Luke x. 20). " The very hairs of your head are all numbered " (Luke xii. 7). " I know whom I have chosen " (John xiii. 18). " I know My sheep, and am known of Mine " (John x. 14). " The Lord knoweth them that are His " (2 Tim. ii. 19). And if the number of these is thus assuredly settled and exactly known, it follows that we are right in asserting—

V.—That the decrees of election and reprobation are immutable and irreversible. Were not this the case—

(1) God's decree would be precarious, frustrable and uncertain, and, by consequence, no decree at all.

(2) His foreknowledge would be wavering, indeterminate, and liable to disappointment, whereas it always has its accomplishment, and necessarily infers the certain futurity of the thing or things foreknown : " I am God, and there is none like Me, declaring the end from the beginning, and, from ancient times, the things that are not yet done ; saying, My counsel shall stand and I will do all My pleasure " (Isa. xlvi. 9, 10).

(3) Neither would His Word be true, which declares that, with regard to the elect, " the gifts and calling of God are without repentance " (Rom. xi. 29) ; that "whom He predestinated, them He also glorified" (Rom. viii. 30) ; that whom He loveth, He loveth to the end (John xiii. 1), with numberless passages to the same purpose. Nor would His word be true with regard to the non-elect if it was possible for them to be saved, for it is there declared that they are fitted for destruction, etc. (Rom. ix. 22) ; foreordained unto condemnation (Jude 4), and delivered over to a reprobate mind in order to their damnation (Rom. i. 28 ; 2 Thess. ii. 12).

G

(4) If, between the elect and reprobate, there was not a great gulph fixed, so that neither can be otherwise than they are, then the will of God (which is the alone cause why some are chosen and others are not) would be rendered inefficacious and of no effect.

(5) Nor could the justice of God stand if He was to condemn the elect, for whose sins He hath received ample satisfaction at the hand of Christ, or if He was to save the reprobate, who are not interested in Christ as the elect are.

(6) The power of God (whereby the elect are preserved from falling into a state of condemnation, and the wicked held down and shut up in a state of death) would be eluded, not to say utterly abolished.

(7) Nor would God be unchangeable if they, who were once the people of His love, could commence the objects of His hatred, or if the vessels of His wrath could be saved with the vessels of grace. Hence that of St. Augustine.* "Brethen," says he, "let us not imagine that God puts down any man in His book and then erases him, for if Pilate could say, 'What I have written, I have written,' how can it be thought that the *great* God would write a person's name in the book of life and then blot it out again?" And may we not, with equal reason, ask, on the other hand, "How can it be thought that any of the reprobate should be written in that book of life, which contains the names of the elect only, or that any should be inscribed there who were not written among the living from eternity?" I shall conclude this chapter with that observation of Luther.† "This," says he, "is the very thing that razes the doctrine of free-will from its foundations, to wit, that God's eternal love of some men and hatred of others is immutable and cannot be reversed." Both one and the other will have its full accomplishment.

---

* Tom. 8, in Psalm 68, col. 738.   † De Serv. Arbitr. cap. 168.

CHAPTER III.

CONCERNING ELECTION UNTO LIFE, OR PREDESTINATION AS IT RESPECTS THE SAINTS IN PARTICULAR.

HAVING considered predestination as it regards all men in general, and briefly shown that by it some are appointed to wrath and others to obtain salvation by Jesus Christ (1 Thess. v. 9), I now come to consider, more distinctly, that branch of it which relates to the saints only, and is commonly styled *election*. Its definition I have given already in the close of the first chapter. What I have farther to advance, from the Scriptures, on this important subject, I shall reduce to several positions, and subjoin a short explanation and confirmation of each.

POSITION 1.—Those who are ordained unto eternal life were not so ordained on account of any worthiness foreseen in them, or of any good works to be wrought by them, nor yet for their future faith, but purely and solely of free, sovereign grace, and according to the mere pleasure of God. This is evident, among other considerations, from this : that faith, repentance and holiness are no less the free-gifts of God than eternal life itself. " Faith—is not of yourselves, it is the gift of God " (Eph. ii. 8). " Unto you it is given to believe " (Phil. i. 29). " Him hath God exalted with His right hand for to give repentance " (Acts v. 31). " Then hath God also to the Gentiles granted repentance unto life " (Acts xi. 18). In like manner holiness is called the sanctification of the Spirit (2 Thess. ii. 13), because the Divine Spirit is the efficient of it in the soul, and, of unholy, makes us holy. Now, if repentance and faith are the gifts, and sanctification is the work of God, then these are not the fruits of man's free-will, nor what he acquires of himself, and so can neither be motives to, nor conditions of his election, which is an act of the Divine mind, antecedent to, and irrespective of all qualities whatever in the persons elected. Besides, the apostle asserts expressly that election is not of works, but of Him that calleth, and that it passed before the persons concerned had done either good or evil (Rom. ix. 11).

Again, if faith or works were the cause of election, God could not be said to choose us, but we to choose Him, contrary to the whole tenor of Scripture : " Ye have not chosen Me, but I have chosen you " (John xv. 16). " Herein is love, not that we loved God, but that He loved us. We love Him because He first loved us " (1 John iv. 10, 19). Election is everywhere asserted to be God's act, and not man's (Mark xiii. 20; Rom. ix. 17; Eph. i. 4; 1 Thess. v. 9; 2 Thess. ii. 13). Once more, we are chosen that we might be holy, not because it was foreseen we would be so (Eph. i. 4), therefore to represent holiness as the reason why we were elected is to make the effect antecedent to the cause. The apostle adds (ver. 5), " having predestinated us according to the good pleasure of His will," most evidently implying that God saw nothing *extra se*, had no motive from without, why He should either choose any at all or this man before another. In a word, the elect were freely loved (Hosea xiv. 4), freely chosen (Rom. xi. 5, 6), and freely redeemed (Isa. lii. 3), they are freely called (2 Tim. i. 9), freely justified (Rom. iii. 24), and shall be freely glorified (Rom. vi. 23). The great Augustine, in his book of Retractations, ingenuously acknowledges his error in having once thought that faith foreseen was a condition of election ; he owns that that opinion is equally impious and absurd, and proves that faith is one of the fruits of election, and consequently could not be, in any sense, a cause of it. " I could never have asserted," says he, " that God in choosing men to life had any respect to their faith, had I duly considered that faith itself is His own gift." And, in another treatise* of his, he has these words : " Since Christ says, ' Ye have not chosen Me,' etc., I would fain ask whether it be Scriptural to say we must

---

* Prædest. cap. 17.

have faith before we are elected, and not, rather, that we are elected in order to our having faith? "

POSITION 2.—As many as are ordained to eternal life are ordained to enjoy that life in and through Christ, and on account of His merits alone (1 Thess. v. 9). Here let it be carefully observed that not the merits of Christ, but the sovereign love of God only is the cause of election itself, but then the merits of Christ are the alone procuring cause of that salvation to which men are elected. This decree of God admits of no cause out of Himself, but the thing decreed, which is the glorification of His chosen ones, may and does admit, nay, necessarily requires, a meritorious cause, which is no other than the obedience and death of Christ.

POSITION 3.—They who are predestinated to life are likewise predestinated to all those means which are indispensably necessary in order to their meetness for, entrance upon, and enjoyment of that life, such as repentance, faith, sanctification, and perseverance in these to the end.

"As many as were ordained to eternal life, believed " (Acts xiii. 48). " He hath chosen us in Him, before the foundation of the world, that we should be holy, and without blame before Him in love " (Eph. i. 4). " For we (*i.e.*, the same we whom He hath chosen before the foundation of the world) are His workmanship, created in Christ Jesus unto good works, which God hath foreordained that we should walk in them " (Eph. ii. 10). And the apostle assures the same Thessalonians, whom he reminds of their election and God's everlasting appointment of them to obtain salvation, that this also was His will concerning them, even their sanctification (1 Thess. i. 4, v. 9, iv. 3), and gives them a view of all these privileges at once. " God hath, from the beginning, chosen you to salvation, through sanctification of the Spirit and belief of the truth " (2 Thess. ii. 13). As does the apostle, "*Elect*—through sanctification of the Spirit *unto* obedience, and sprinkling of the blood of

Jesus Christ '' (1 Peter i. 2). Now, though faith and holiness are not represented as the cause wherefore the elect are saved, yet these are constantly represented as the means through which they are saved, or as the appointed way wherein God leads His people to glory, these blessings being always bestowed previous to that. Agreeable to all which is that of Augustine :* '' Whatsoever persons are, through the riches of Divine grace, exempted from the original sentence of condemnation are undoubtedly brought to hear the Gospel,† and when heard, they are caused to believe it, and are made likewise to endure to the end in the faith which works by love, and should they at any time go astray, they are recovered and set right again.'' A little after he adds : ''All these things are wrought in them by that God who made them vessels of mercy, and who, by the election of His grace, chose them, in His Son, before the world began.''

POSITION 4.—Not one of the elect can perish, but they must all necessarily be saved. The reason is this : because God simply and unchangeably wills that all and every one of those whom He hath appointed to life should be eternally glorified, and, as was observed towards the end of the preceding chapter, all the Divine attributes are concerned in the accomplishment of this His will. His wisdom, which cannot err ; His knowledge, which cannot be deceived ; His truth, which cannot fail ; His love, which nothing can alienate ; His justice, which cannot condemn any for whom Christ died ; His power, which none can resist ; and His unchangeableness, which can never vary—from all which it appears that we do not speak at all improperly when we say that the salvation of His people is necessary and certain. Now that is said to be necessary (*quod nequit aliter esse*) which cannot be otherwise than it is, and if all the perfections

---

* De Corrept. et Grat. cap. 7.

† We must understand this, in a qualified sense, as intending that all those of the elect, who live where the Christian dispensation obtains, are, sooner or later, brought to hear the Gospel, and to believe it.

of God are engaged to preserve and save His children, their safety and salvation must be, in the strictest sense of the word, necessary. (See Psalm ciii. 17, cxxv. 1, 2; Isa. xlv. 17, liv. 9, 10; Jer. xxxi. 38, xxxii. 40; John vi. 39, x. 28, 29, xiv. 19, xvii. 12; Rom. viii. 30, 38, 39, xi. 29; 1 Cor. i. 8, 9; Phil. i. 6; 1 Peter i. 4, 5).

Thus St. Augustine :* "Of those whom God hath predestinated none can perish, inasmuch as they are His own elect," and ib., "They are the elect who are predestinated, foreknown, and called according to purpose. Now, could any of these be lost, God would be disappointed of His will and expectation; but He cannot be so disappointed, therefore they can never perish. Again, could they be lost, the power of God would be made void by man's sin, but His power is invincible, therefore they are safe." And again (chap. 9), "The children of God are written, with an unshaken stability, in the book of their heavenly Father's remembrance." And in the same chapter he hath these words : "Not the children of promise, but the children of perdition shall perish, for the former are the predestinated, who are called according to the Divine determination, not one of whom shall finally miscarry." So likewise Luther :† "God's decree of predestination is firm and certain, and the necessity resulting from it is, in like manner, immoveable, and cannot but take place. For we ourselves are so feeble that, if the matter was left in our hands, very few, or rather none, would be saved, but Satan would overcome us all." To which he adds : "Now, since this steadfast and inevitable purpose of God cannot be reversed nor disannulled by any creature whatever, we have a most assured hope that we shall finally triumph over sin, how violently soever it may at present rage in our mortal bodies."

POSITION 5.—The salvation of the elect was not the only nor yet the principal end of their being chosen, but

---

* Tom. 7, De Corr. et Grat. cap. 7.   † In Præfat. ad Epist. ad Rom.

God's grand end, in appointing them to life and happiness, was to display the riches of His own mercy, and that He might be glorified in and by the persons He had thus chosen.

For this reason the elect are styled vessels of mercy, because they were originally created, and afterwards by the Divine Spirit created anew, with this design and to this very end, that the sovereignty of the Father's grace, the freeness of His love, and the abundance of His goodness might be manifested in their eternal happiness. Now God, as we have already more than once had occasion to observe, does nothing in time which He did not from eternity resolve within Himself to do, and if He, in time, creates and regenerates His people with a view to display His unbounded mercy, He must consequently have decreed from all eternity to do this with the same view. So that the final causes of election appear to be these two : first and principally, the glory* of God ; second and subordinately, the salvation of those He has elected, from which the former arises, and by which it is illustrated and set off. So, " The Lord hath made all things for Himself " (Prov. xvi. 1), and hence that of Paul, " He hath chosen us—to the praise of the glory of His grace " (Eph. i.).

POSITION 6.—The end of election, which, with regard to the elect themselves, is eternal life. I say this end and the means conducive to it, such as the gift of the Spirit, faith, etc., are so inseparably connected together that whoever is possessed of these shall surely obtain that,

---

* Let it be carefully observed that when with the Scriptures we assert the glory of God to be the ultimate end of His dealings with angels and men, we do not speak this with respect to His essential glory which He has as God, and which, as it is infinite, is not susceptible of addition nor capable of diminution, but of that glory which is purely manifestative, and which Micrælius, in his Lexic. Philosoph. col. 471, defines to be, *Clara rei cum laude notitia ; cum nempe, ipsa sua eminentia est magna, augusta, et conspicua.* And the accurate Maestricht, *Celebratio ceu manifestatio (quæ magis proprie glorificatio, quam gloria appellatur), qua, agnita intus eminentia, ejusque congrua æstimatio, propalatur et extollitur.*—Theolog. lib. 2, cap. 22 § 8.

and none can obtain that who are not first possessed of
these. "As many as were ordained to eternal life," and
none else, "believed" (Acts xiii. 48). "Him hath God
exalted—to give repentance unto Israel and remission of
sins" (Acts v. 31) : not to all men, or to those who were
not, in the counsel and purpose of God, set apart for
Himself, but to Israel, all His chosen people, who were
given to Him, were ransomed by Him, and shall be saved
in Him with an everlasting salvation. "According to the
faith of God's elect" (Tit. i. 1), so that true faith is a
consequence of election, is peculiar to the elect, and shall
issue in life eternal. "He hath chosen us—that we should
be holy" (Eph. i.), therefore all who are chosen are
made holy, and none but they ; and all who are sanctified
have a right to believe they were elected, and that they
shall assuredly be saved. "Whom He did predestinate,
them He also called; whom He called, them He also
justified ; and whom He justified, them He also glorified"
(Rom. viii. 30), which shows that effectual calling and
justification are indissolubly connected with election on
one hand and eternal happiness on the other ; that they
are a proof of the former and an earnest of the latter.
"Ye believe not, because ye are not of My sheep" (John
x. 26) ; on the contrary, they who believe, therefore,
believe because they are of His sheep. Faith, then, is
an evidence of election, or of being in the number of
Christ's sheep ; consequently, of salvation, since all His
sheep shall be saved (John x. 28).

POSITION 7.—The elect may, through the grace of
God, attain to the knowledge and assurance of their predestination to life, and they ought to seek after it. The
Christian may, for instance, argue thus : " 'As many as
were ordained to eternal life, believed' ; through mercy
I believe, therefore, I am ordained to eternal life. 'He
that believeth shall be saved' ; I believe, therefore, I am
in a saved state. 'Whom He did predestinate, He
called, justified and glorified' ; I have reason to trust
that He hath called and justified ME ; therefore I can

assuredly look backward on my eternal predestination, and forward to my certain glorification." To all which frequently accedes the immediate testimony of the Divine Spirit witnessing with the believer's conscience that he is a child of God (Rom. viii. 16 ; Gal. iv. 6 ; 1 John v. 10). Christ forbids His little flock to fear, inasmuch as they might, on good and solid grounds, rest satisfied and assured that "it is the Father's" unalterable "good pleasure to give them the kingdom" (Luke xii. 32). And this was the faith of the apostle (Rom. viii. 38, 39).

POSITION 8.—The true believer ought not only to be thoroughly established in the point of his own election, but should likewise believe the election of all his other fellow-believers and brethren in Christ. Now, as there are most evident and indubitable marks of election laid down in Scripture, a child of God, by examining himself whether those marks are found on him, may arrive at a sober and well-grounded certainty of his own particular interest in that unspeakable privilege ; and by the same rule whereby he judges of himself he may likewise (but with caution) judge of others. If I see the external fruits and criteria of election on this or that man, I may reasonably, and in a judgment of charity, conclude such an one to be an elect person. So St. Paul, · beholding the gracious fruits which appeared in the believing Thessalonians, gathered from thence that they were elected of God (1 Thess. i. 4, 5), and knew also the election of the Christian Ephesians (Eph. i. 4, 5), as Peter also did that of the members of the churches in Pontus, Galatia, etc. (1 Peter i. 2). It is true, indeed, that all conclusions of this nature are not now infallible, but our judgments are liable to mistake, and God only, whose is the book of life, and who is the Searcher of hearts, can absolutely know them that are His (2 Tim. ii. 19) ; yet we may, without a presumptuous intrusion into things not seen, arrive at a moral certainty in this matter. And I cannot see how Christian love can be cultivated, how we can call one another brethren in the Lord, or how believers can hold religious fellowship and communion with each other, unless they have some solid and visible reason to conclude that they are loved with the same everlasting love, were redeemed by the same Saviour, are partakers of like grace, and shall reign in the same glory.

But here let me suggest one very necessary caution, viz., that though we may, at least very probably, infer the election of some persons from the marks and appearances of grace which may be discoverable in them, yet we can never judge any man whatever to be a reprobate. That there are reprobate persons is very evident from Scripture (as we shall presently show), but who they are is known alone to Him, who alone can tell who and what men are not written in the Lamb's book of life. I grant that there are some particular persons mentioned in the Divine Word of whose reprobation no doubt can be made, such as Esau and Judas; but now the canon of Scripture is completed, we dare not, we must not pronounce any man living to be non-elect, be he at present ever so wicked. The vilest sinner may, for aught we can tell, appertain to the election of grace, and be one day wrought upon by the Spirit of God. This we know, that those who die in unbelief and are finally unsanctified cannot be saved, because God in His Word tells us so, and has represented these as marks of reprobation; but to say that such and such individuals, whom, perhaps, we now see dead in sins, shall never be converted to Christ, would be a most presumptuous assertion, as well as an inexcusable breach of the charity which hopeth all things.

CHAPTER IV.

OF REPROBATION OR PREDESTINATION AS IT RESPECTS THE UNGODLY.

FROM what has been said in the preceding chapter concerning the election of some, it would unavoidably follow, even supposing the Scriptures had been silent about it, that there must be a rejection of others, as every choice does, most evidently and necessarily, imply a refusal, for where there is no leaving out there can be no choice. But beside the testimony of reason, the Divine Word is full and express to our purpose; it frequently, and in terms too clear to be misunderstood, and too strong to be evaded by any who are not proof against the most cogent evidence, attests this tremendous truth, that some are " of old fore-ordained to condemnation." I shall, in the discussion of this awful subject, follow the method hitherto observed, and throw what I have to say into several distinct positions supported by Scripture.

POSITION 1.—God did, from all eternity, decree to leave some of Adam's fallen posterity in their sins, and to exclude them from the participation of Christ and His benefits. For the clearing of this, let it be observed that in all ages the much greater part of mankind have been destitute even of the external means of grace, and have not been favoured with the preaching of God's Word or any revelation of His will. Thus, anciently, the Jews, who were in number the fewest of all people, were, nevertheless, for a long series of ages, the only nation to whom the Deity was pleased to make any special discovery of Himself, and it is observable that our Lord Himself principally confined the advantages of His public ministry to that people; nay, He forbade His disciples to go among any others (Matt. x. 5, 6), and did not commission them to preach the Gospel indiscriminately to Jews and Gentiles until after His resurrection (Mark xvi. 15; Luke xxiv. 47). Hence many nations and communities never had the advantage of hearing the Word preached, and consequently were strangers to the faith that cometh thereby.

It is not indeed improbable, but some individuals in these unenlightened countries might belong to the secret election of grace, and the habit of faith might be wrought in these. However, be that as it will, our argument is not affected by it. It is evident that the nations of the world were generally ignorant, not only of God Himself, but likewise of the way to please Him, the true manner of acceptance with Him, and the means of arriving at the everlasting enjoyment of Him. Now, if God had been pleased to have saved those people, would He not have vouchsafed them the ordinary means of salvation? Would He not have given them all things necessary in order to that end? But it is undeniable matter of fact that He did not, and to very many nations of the earth does not at this day. If, then, the Deity can consistently with His attributes deny to some the means of grace, and shut them up in gross darkness and unbelief, why should it be thought incompatible with His immensely glorious perfections to exclude some persons from grace itself, and from that eternal life which is connected with it, especially seeing He is equally the Lord and sovereign Disposer of the end to which the means lead, as of the means which lead to that end? Both one and the other are His, and He most justly may, as He most assuredly will, do what He pleases with His own.

Besides, it being also evident that many, even of them who live in places where the Gospel is preached, as well as of those among whom it never was preached, die strangers to God and holiness, and without experiencing anything of the gracious influences of His Spirit, we may reasonably and safely conclude that one cause of their so dying is because it was not the Divine will to communicate His grace unto them, since, had it been His will, He would actually have made them partakers thereof, and had they been partakers of it they could not have died without it. Now, if it was the will of God in time to refuse them this grace, it must have been His will from eternity, since His will is, as Himself, the same yesterday, to-day, and for ever.

The actions of God being thus fruits of His eternal purpose, we may safely, and without any danger of mistake, argue from them to that and infer that God therefore does such and such things, because He decreed to

do them, His own will being the sole cause of all His
works. So that, from His actually leaving some men in
final impenitency and unbelief, we assuredly gather that
it was His everlasting determination so to do, and consequently that He reprobated some from before the
foundation of the world. And as this inference is strictly
rational, so is it perfectly Scriptural. Thus the Judge
will in the last day declare to those on the left hand,
" I never knew you " (Matt. vii. 23), *i.e.*, " I never, no,
not from eternity, loved, approved or acknowledged you
for Mine," or, in other words, " I always hated you."

Our Lord (in John xvii.) divides the whole human
race into two great classes—one He calls the world ; the
other, " the men who were given Him out of the world."
The latter, it is said, the Father loved, even as He loved
Christ Himself (ver. 23), but He loved Christ " before
the foundation of the world " (ver. 24), *i.e.*, from everlasting ; therefore He loved the elect so too, and if He
loved these from eternity, it follows, by all the rules of
antithesis, that He hated the others as early. So, " The
children being not yet born, neither having done good
or evil, that the purpose of God," etc. (Rom. ix.). From
the example of the two twins, Jacob and Esau, the apostle
infers the eternal election of some men and the eternal
rejection of all the rest.

POSITION 2.—Some men were, from all eternity, not
only negatively excepted from a participation of Christ
and His salvation, but positively ordained to continue in
their natural blindness, hardness of heart, etc., and that
by the just judgment of God. (See Exod. ix. ; 1 Sam.
ii. 25 ; 2 Sam. xvii. 14 ; Isa. vi. 9-11 ; 2 Thess. ii. 11, 12.)
Nor can these places of Scripture, with many others of
like import, be understood of an involuntary permission
on the part of God, as if God barely suffered it to be so,
quasi invitus, as it were by constraint, and against His
will, for He permits nothing which He did not resolve
and determine to permit. His permission is a positive,
determinate act of His will, as Augustine, Luther and

Bucer justly observe. Therefore, if it be the will of God in time to permit such and such men to continue in their natural state of ignorance and corruption, the natural consequence of which is their falling into such and such sins (observe God does not force them into sin, their actual disobedience being only the consequence of their not having that grace which God is not obliged to grant them)—I say, if it be the will of God thus to leave them in time (and we must deny demonstration itself, even known absolute matter of fact, if we deny that some are so left), then it must have been the Divine intention from all eternity so to leave them, since, as we have already had occasion to observe, no new will can possibly arise in the mind of God. We see that evil men actually are suffered to go on adding sin to sin, and if it be not inconsistent with the sacred attributes actually to permit this, it could not possibly be inconsistent with them to decree that permission before the foundations of the world were laid.

Thus God efficaciously permitted (having so decreed) the Jews to be, in effect, the crucifiers of Christ, and Judas to betray Him (Acts iv. 27, 28 ; Matt. xxvi. 23, 24). Hence we find St. Augustine* speaking thus : " Judas was chosen, but it was to do a most execrable deed, that thereby the death of Christ, and the adorable work of redemption by Him, might be accomplished. When therefore we hear our Lord say, ' Have not I chosen you twelve, and one of you is a devil? ' we must understand it thus, that the eleven were chosen in mercy, but Judas in judgment ; they were chosen to partake of Christ's kingdom ; he was chosen and pitched upon to betray Him and be the means of shedding His blood."

POSITION 3.—The non-elect were predestinated, not only to continue in final impenitency, sin and unbelief, but were likewise, for such their sins, righteously appointed to infernal death hereafter.

---

* De Corr. and Grat. cap. 7.

This position is also self-evident, for it is certain that in the day of universal judgment all the human race will not be admitted into glory, but some of them transmitted to the place of torment. Now, God does and will do nothing but in consequence of His own decree (Psalm cxxxv. 6; Isa. xlvi. 11; Eph. i. 9, 11); therefore the condemnation of the unrighteous was decreed of God, and if decreed by Him, decreed from everlasting, for all His decrees are eternal. Besides, if God purposed to leave those persons under the guilt and the power of sin, their condemnation must of itself necessarily follow, since without justification and sanctification (neither of which blessings are in the power of man) none can enter heaven (John xiii. 8; Heb. xii. 14). Therefore, if God determined within Himself thus to leave some in their sins (and it is but too evident that this is really the case), He must also have determined within Himself to punish them for those sins (final guilt and final punishment being correlatives which necessarily infer each other), but God did determine both to leave and to punish the non-elect, therefore there was a reprobation of some from eternity. Thus, " Go, ye cursed, into everlasting fire, prepared for the devil and his angels " (Matt. xxv.); for Satan and all his messengers, emissaries and imitators, whether apostate spirits or apostate men.

Now, if penal fire was, in decree from everlasting, prepared for them, they, by all the laws of argument in the world, must have been in the counsel of God prepared, *i.e.*, designed for that fire, which is the point I undertook to prove. Hence we read " of vessels of wrath fitted to destruction, κατηρτισμένα εις ἀπώλειαν, put together, made up, formed or fashioned, for perdition " (Rom. ix.), who are and can be no other than the reprobate. To multiply Scriptures on this head would be almost endless; for a sample, consult Prov. xvi. 4; 1 Peter ii. 8; 2 Peter ii. 12; Jude 4; Rev. xiii. 8.

POSITION 4.—As the future faith and good works of the elect were not the cause of their being chosen, so neither were the future sins of the reprobate the cause of their being passed by, but both the choice of the former and the decretive omission of the latter were owing, merely and entirely, to the sovereign will and determinating pleasure of God.

We distinguish between preterition, or bare non-election, which is a purely negative thing, and condemnation, or appointment to punishment : the will of God was the cause of the former, the sins of the non-elect are the reason of the latter. Though God determined to leave, and actually does leave, whom He pleases in the spiritual darkness and death of nature, out of which He is under no obligation to deliver them, yet He does not positively condemn any of these merely because He hath not chosen them, but because they have sinned against Him. (See Rom. i. 21-24; Rom. ii. 8, 9; 2 Thess. ii. 12.) Their preterition or non-inscription in the book of life is not unjust on the part of God, because out of a world of rebels, equally involved in guilt, God (who might, without any impeachment of His justice, have passed by all, as He did the reprobate angels) was, most unquestionably, at liberty, if it so pleased Him, to extend the sceptre of His clemency to some and to pitch upon whom He would as the objects of it. Nor was this exemption of some any injury to the non-elect, whose case would have been just as bad as it is, even supposing the others had not been chosen at all. Again, the condemnation of the ungodly (for it is under that character alone that they are the subjects of punishment and were ordained to it) is not unjust, seeing it is for sin and only for sin. None are or will be punished but for their iniquities, and all iniquity is properly meritorious of punishment : where, then, is the supposed unmercifulness, tyranny or injustice of the Divine procedure?

POSITION 5.—God is the creator of the wicked, but not of their wickedness; He is the author of their being, but not the infuser of their sin.

It is most certainly His will (for adorable and un-

H

searchable reasons) to permit sin, but, with all possible
reverence be it spoken, it should seem that He cannot,
consistently with the purity of His nature, the glory of
His attributes, and the truth of His declarations, be
Himself the author of it. "Sin," says the apostle,
"entered into the world by one man," meaning by Adam,
consequently it was not introduced by the Deity Himself.
Though without the permission of His will and the con-
currence of His providence, its introduction had been
impossible, yet is He not hereby the Author of sin so
introduced.* Luther observes (*De Serv. Arb.*, c. 42):
"It is a great degree of faith to believe that God is
merciful and gracious, though He saves so few and condemns so many, and that He is strictly just, though,
in consequence of His own will, He made us not exempt
from liableness to condemnation." And cap. 148:
"Although God doth not make sin, nevertheless He ceases
not to create and multiply individuals in the human
nature, which, through the withholding of His Spirit, is
corrupted by sin, just as a skilful artist may form curious
statues out of bad materials. So, such as their nature is,
such are men themselves; God forms them out of such
a nature."

POSITION 6.—The condemnation of the reprobate is
necessary and inevitable. Which we prove thus. It is
evident from Scripture that the reprobate shall be condemned. But nothing comes to pass (much less can the

---

* It is a known and very just maxim of the schools, *Effectus sequitur
causam proximam:* "An effect follows from, and is to be inscribed to,
the last immediate cause that produced it." Thus, for instance, if I
hold a book or a stone in my hand, my holding it is the immediate cause
of its not falling; but if I let it go, my letting it go is not the immediate
cause of its falling: it is carried downwards by its own gravity, which
is therefore the *causa proxima effectus*, the proper and immediate cause
of its descent. It is true, if I had kept my hold of it, it would not have
fallen, yet still the immediate, direct cause of its fall is its own weight,
not my quitting my hold. The application of this to the providence of
God, as concerned in sinful events, is easy. Without God, there could
have been no creation; without creation, no creatures; without creatures,
no sin. Yet is not sin chargeable on God: for *effectus sequitur causam
proximam.*

condemnation of a rational creature) but in consequence of the will and decree of God. Therefore the non-elect could not be condemned was it not the Divine pleasure and determination that they should, and if God wills and determines their condemnation, that condemnation is necessary and inevitable. By their sins they have made themselves guilty of death, and as it is not the will of God to pardon those sins and grant them repentance unto life, the punishment of such impenitent sinners is as unavoidable as it is just. It is our Lord's own declaration that " a corrupt tree cannot bring forth good fruit " (Matt. vii.), or, in other words, that a depraved sinner cannot produce in himself those gracious habits, nor exert those gracious acts, without which no adult person can be saved. Consequently the reprobate must, as corrupt, fruitless trees (or fruitful in evil only), be " hewn down and cast into the fire " (Matt. iii.). This, therefore, serves as another argument in proof of the inevitability of their future punishment, which argument, in brief, amounts to this : they who are not saved from sin must unavoidably perish, but the reprobate are not saved from sin (for they have neither will nor power to save themselves, and God, though He certainly can, yet He certainly will not save them), therefore their perdition is unavoidable. Nor does it follow, from hence, that God forces the reprobate into sin, and thereby into misery, against their wills, but that, in consequence of their natural depravity (which it is not the Divine pleasure to deliver them out of, neither is He bound to do it, nor are they themselves so much as desirous that He would), they are voluntarily biassed and inclined to evil; nay, which is worse still, they hug and value their spiritual chains, and even greedily pursue the paths of sin, which lead to the chambers of death. Thus God does not (as we are slanderously reported to affirm) compel the wicked to sin, as the rider spurs forward an unwilling horse; God only says in effect that tremendous word, " Let them alone " (Matt. xv. 14). He need but slacken the

reins of providential restraint and withhold the influence
of saving grace, and apostate man will too soon, and too
surely, of his own accord, " fall by his iniquity " ; he will
presently be, spiritually speaking, a *felo de se*, and,
without any other efficiency, lay violent hands on his
own soul. So that though the condemnation of the
reprobate is unavoidable, yet the necessity of it is so far
from making them mere machines or involuntary agents,
that it does not in the least interfere with the rational
freedom of their wills, nor serve to render them less
inexcusable.

POSITION 7.—The punishment of the non-elect was
not the ultimate end of their creation, but the glory of
God. It is frequently objected to us that, according to
our view of predestination, " God makes some persons
on purpose to damn them," but this we never advanced ;
nay, we utterly reject it as equally unworthy of God to
do and of a rational being to suppose. The grand, principal end, proposed by the Deity to Himself in His for-
mation of all things, and of mankind in particular, was
the manifestation and display of His own glorious attributes. His ultimate scope in the creation of the elect
is to evidence and make known by their salvation the
unsearchable riches of His power and wisdom, mercy and
love, and the creation of the non-elect is for the display
of His justice, power, sovereignty, holiness and truth.
So that nothing can be more certain than the declaration
of the text we have frequently had occasion to cite, " The
Lord hath made all things for Himself, even the wicked
for the day of evil " (Prov. xvi.). On one hand, the
" vessels of wrath are fitted for destruction," in order
that God may " show His wrath and make His power
known," and manifest the greatness of His patience and
longsuffering (Rom. ix. 32). On the other hand, He afore
prepared the elect to salvation, that on them He might
demonstrate "the riches of His glory and mercy" (ver. 23).
As, therefore, God Himself is the sole Author and efficient
of all His own actions, so is He likewise the supreme end
to which they lead and in which they terminate.

Besides, the creation and perdition of the ungodly answer another purpose (though a subordinate one) with regard to the elect themselves, who from the rejection of those learn (1) to admire the riches of the Divine love toward themselves, which planned and has accomplished the work of their salvation, while others, by nature on an equal level with them, are excluded from a participation of the same benefits. And such a view of the Lord's distinguishing mercy is (2) a most powerful motive to thankfulness that when they too might justly have been condemned with the world of the non-elect, they were marked out as heirs of the grace of life. (3) Hereby they are taught ardently to love their heavenly Father; (4) to trust in Him assuredly for a continued supply of grace while they are on earth. and for the accomplishment of His eternal decree and promise by their glorification in heaven; and (5) to live as becomes those who have received such unspeakable mercies from the hand of their God and Saviour. So Bucer somewhere observes that the punishment of the reprobate "is useful to the elect, inasmuch as it influences them to a greater fear and abhorrence of sin, and to a firmer reliance on the goodness of God."

Position 8.—Notwithstanding God did from all eternity irreversibly choose out and fix upon some to be partakers of salvation by Christ and rejected the rest (who are therefore termed by the apostle,. οἱ λοιποί, the refuse, or those that remained and were left out), acting in both according to the good pleasure of His own sovereign will, yet He did not herein act an unjust, tyrannical or cruel part, nor yet show Himself a respecter of persons

(1) He is not unjust in reprobating some, neither can He be so, for "the Lord is holy in all His ways and righteous in all His works" (Psa. cxlv.). But salvation and damnation are works of His, consequently neither of them is unrighteous or unholy. It is undoubted matter of fact that the Father draws some men to Christ and saves them in Him with an everlasting salvation, and

that He neither draws nor saves some others; and if it be
not unjust in God actually to forbear saving these persons
after they are born, it could not be unjust in Him to
determine as much before they were born. What is not
unjust for God to do in time, could not, by parity of
argument, be unjust in Him to resolve upon and decree
from eternity. And, surely, if the apostle's illustration
be allowed to have any propriety, or to carry any authority, it can no more be unjust in God to set apart some
for communion with Himself in this life and the next,
and to set aside others according to His own free pleasure,
than for a potter to make out of the same mass of clay
some vessels for honourable and others for inferior uses.
The Deity, being absolute Lord of all His creatures, is
accountable to none for His doings, and cannot be chargeable with injustice for disposing of His own as He will.

(2) Nor is the decree of reprobation a tyrannical one.
It is, indeed, strictly sovereign; but lawful sovereignty
and lawless tyranny are as really distinct and different
as any two opposites can be. He is a tyrant, in the
common acceptation of that word, who (a) either usurps
the sovereign authority and arrogates to himself a
dominion to which he has no right, or (b) who, being
originally a lawful prince, abuses his power and governs
contrary to law. But who dares to lay either of these
accusations to the Divine charge? God as Creator has a
most unquestionable and unlimited right over the souls
and bodies of men, unless it can be supposed, contrary to
all Scripture and common sense, that in making of man
He made a set of beings superior to Himself and exempt
from His jurisdiction. Taking it for granted, therefore,
that God has an absolute right of sovereignty over His
creatures, if He should be pleased (as the Scriptures
repeatedly assure us that He is) to manifest and display
that right by graciously saving some and justly punishing
others for their sins, who are we that we should reply
against God?

Neither does the ever-blessed Deity fall under the

second notion of a tyrant, namely, as one who abuses his power by acting contrary to law, for by what exterior law is HE bound, who is the supreme Law-giver of the universe? The laws promulgated by Him are designed for the rule of our conduct, not of His. Should it be objected that '' His own attributes of goodness and justice, holiness and truth, are a law to Himself,'' I answer that, admitting this to be the case, there is nothing in the decree of reprobation as represented in Scripture, and by us from thence, which clashes with any of those perfections. With regard to the Divine goodness, though the non-elect are not objects of it in the sense the elect are, yet even they are not wholly excluded from a participation of it. They enjoy the good things of providence in common with God's children, and very often in a much higher degree. Besides, goodness, considered as it is in God, would have been just the same infinite and glorious attribute, supposing no rational beings had been created at all or saved when created. To which may be added, that the goodness of the Deity does not cease to be infinite in itself, only because it is more extended to some objects than it is to others. The infinity of this perfection, as residing in God and coinciding with His essence, is sufficiently secured, without supposing it to reach indiscriminately to all the creatures He has made. For, was this way of reasoning to be admitted, it would lead us too far and prove too much, since, if the infinity of His goodness is to be estimated by the number of objects upon which it terminates, there must be an absolute, proper infinity of reasonable beings to terminate that goodness upon; consequently it would follow from such premises either that the creation is as truly infinite as the Creator, or, if otherwise, that the Creator's goodness could not be infinite, because it has not an infinity of objects to make happy.*

---

* The late most learned and judicious Mr. Charnock has, in my judgment at least, proved most clearly and satisfactorily that the exclusion of some individual persons from a participation of saving grace

Lastly, if it was not incompatible with God's infinite goodness to pass by the whole body of fallen angels and leave them under the guilt of their apostacy, much less can it clash with that attribute to pass by some of fallen mankind and resolve to leave them in their sins and punish them for them. Nor is it inconsistent with Divine justice to withhold saving grace from some, seeing the grace of God is not what He owes to any. It is a free gift to those that have it, and is not due to those that are

---

is perfectly consistent with God's unlimited goodness. He observes that " the goodness of the Deity is infinite and circumscribed by no limits. The exercise of His goodness may be limited by Himself, but His goodness, the principle, cannot, for, since His essence is infinite, and His goodness is not distinguished from His essence, it is infinite also. God is necessarily good in His nature, but free in His communications of it. He is necessarily good, *affective*, in regard of His nature, but freely good, *effective*, in regard of the effluxes of it to this or that particular subject He pitcheth upon. He is not necessarily communicative of His goodness, as the sun of its light or a tree of its cooling shade, which chooses not its objects, but enlightens all indifferently without variation or distinction : this were to make God of no more understanding than the sun, which shines not where it pleases, but where it must. He is an understanding agent, and hath a sovereign right to choose His own subjects. It would not be a supreme if it were not a voluntary goodness. It is agreeable to the nature of the Highest Good to be absolutely free, and to dispense His goodness in what methods and measures He pleases, according to the free determinations of His own will, guided by the wisdom of His mind and regulated by the holiness of His nature. He will be good to whom He will be good. When He doth act, He cannot but act well; so far it is necessary : yet He may act this good or that good, to this or that degree; so it is free. As it is the perfection of His nature, it is necessary; as it is the communication of His bounty, it is voluntary. The eye cannot but see if it be open, yet it may glance on this or that colour, fix upon this or that object, as it is conducted by the will. What necessity could there be on God to resolve to communicate His goodness [at all]? It could not be to make Himself better by it, for he had [before] a goodness incapable of any addition. What obligation could there be from the creature? Whatever sparks of goodness any creature hath are the free effusions of God's bounty, the off-springs of his own inclination to do well, the simple favour of the donor. God is as unconstrained in His liberty in all His communications as [He is] infinite in His goodness the fountain of them."—Charnock's Works, Vol. 1, p. 583, etc. With whom agrees the excellent Dr. Bates, surnamed, for his eloquence, the silver-tongued, and who, if he had a silver tongue, had likewise a golden pen. " God," says he, " is a wise and free agent, and as He is infinite in goodness, so the exercise of it is voluntary, and only so far as He pleases."—Harm. of Divine Attrib., chap. 3.

without it; consequently there can be no injustice in not giving what God is not bound to bestow. There is no end of cavilling at the Divine dispensations if men are disposed to do it. We might, with equality of reason, when our hand is in, presume to charge the Deity with partiality for not making all His creatures angels because it was in His power to do so, as charge Him with injustice for not electing all mankind. Besides, how can it possibly be subversive of His justice to condemn, and resolve to condemn, the non-elect for their sins when those very sins were not atoned for by Christ as the sins of the elect were? His justice in this case is so far from hindering the condemnation of the reprobate that it renders it necessary and indispensable. Again, is the decree of sovereign preterition and of just condemnation for sin repugnant to the Divine holiness? Not in the least, so far from it, that it does not appear how the Deity could be holy if He did not hate sin and punish it. Neither is it contrary to His truth and veracity. Quite the reverse. For would not the Divine veracity fall to the ground if the finally wicked were not condemned?

(3) God, in the reprobation of some, does not act a cruel part. Whoever accused a chief magistrate of cruelty for not sparing a company of atrocious malefactors, and for letting the sentence of the law take place upon them by their execution? If, indeed, the magistrate pleases to pity some of them and remit their penalty, we applaud his clemency, but the punishment of the rest is no impeachment of his mercy. Now, with regard to God, His mercy is free and voluntary. He may extend it to and withhold it from whom He pleases (Rom. ix. 15, 18), and it is sad indeed if we will not allow the Sovereign, the all-wise Governor of heaven and earth, the same privilege and liberty we allow to a supreme magistrate below.

(4) Nor is God, in choosing some and rejecting others, a respecter of persons. He only comes under that title who, on account of parentage, country, dignity, wealth,

or for any other external consideration,* shows more
favour to one person than to another. But that is not
the case with God. He considers all men as sinners by
nature, and has compassion not on persons of this or that
sect, country, sex, age or station in life, because they are
so circumstanced, but on whom, and because, He will have

---

* προσωπολημψια, *Personæ acceptio, quum magis huic favemus,
quam illi, ob circumstantiam aliquam, ceu qualitatem, externam, ei
adhærentem; puta genus, dignitatem, opes, patriam, etc.* Scapula, in voc.
So that elegant, accurate and learned Dutch divine, Laurentius:
*Hæc vero [i.e., προσωπολημψια] est, quando persona personæ præfertur
ex causa indebita: puta, si judex absolvat reum, vel quia dives est, vel
quia potens, vel quia magistratus est, vel quia amicus et propinquus est,
etc.* " That is respect of persons, when one man is preferred to another
on some sinister and undue account, as when a judge acquits a criminal
merely because he is rich, or powerful, or is his friend or relation, etc."—
Comment. in Epist. Jacob, p. 92.
Now, in the matter of election and preterition, God is influenced by
no such motives, nor indeed by any exterior inducement or any motive,
extra se, out of Himself. He does not, for instance, condemn any
persons on account of their poverty, but, on the reverse, hath chosen
many who are poor in this world (James ii. 5): Nor does He condemn
any for being rich, for some, even of the mighty and noble, are called
by His grace (1 Cor. i. 26). He does not respect any man's parentage
or country, for the elect will be " gathered together from the four winds,
from under one end of heaven to the other " (Matt. xxiv. 31), and He
hath redeemed to Himself a select number " out of every kindred and
tongue, and people, and nation " (Rev. v. 9; vii. 9). So far is God
from being in any sense a respecter of persons, that in Christ Jesus,
there is neither Jew nor Greek, bond nor free, male nor female (Gal.
iii. 28). He does not receive one nor reject another merely for coming
or not coming under any of these characters. His own sovereign will,
and not their external or internal circumstances, was the sole rule by
which He proceeded in appointing some to salvation and decreeing to
leave others in their sins. So that God is not herein a respecter of their
persons, but a respecter of Himself and His own glory.
And as God is no respecter of persons because He chooses some as
objects of His favour and omits others, all being on a perfect equality,
so neither does it follow that He is such from His actually conferring
spiritual and eternal blessings on the former and denying them to the
latter, seeing these blessings are absolutely His own, and which He
may, therefore, without injustice, give or not give at His pleasure.
Dr. Whitby himself, though so strenuous an adversary to everything
that looks like predestination, yet very justly observes (and such a
concession from such a pen merits the reader's attention): " Locum non
habet [scil. προσωπολημψια] in bonis mere liberis et gratuitis: neque in
iis. in quibus, unum alteri præferre, nostri arbitrii out privilegii est."—
Ethic. Compend., 1. 2, c. 5, sect. 9, *i.e.*, " The bestowing [and consequently the withholding] of such benefits, as are merely gratuitous

compassion. Pertinent to the present purpose is that passage of St. Augustine :* " Forasmuch as some people imagine that they must look on God as a respecter of persons if they believe that without any respect had to the previous merits of men, He hath mercy on whom He will, and calls whom it is His pleasure to call, and makes good whom He pleases. The scrupulousness of such people arises from their not duly attending to this one thing, namely, that damnation is rendered to the wicked as a matter of debt, justice and desert, whereas the grace given to those who are delivered is free and unmerited,

and undeserved, does not argue respect of persons ; neither is it respect of persons to prefer one before another when we have a right and it is our pleasure so to do."

I shall only add the testimony of Thomas Aquinas, a man of some genius and much application, who, though in very many things a laborious trifler, was yet, on some subjects, a clear reasoner and judicious writer. His words are : " Duplex est datio ; una quidem pertinens ad justitiam ; qua scilicet, aliquis dat alicui quod ei debetur ; et circa tales dationes attenditur personarum acceptio. Alia est datio ad liberalitatem pertinens ; qua, scilicet, gratis datur alicui quod ei non debetur. Et talis est Collatio munerum gratiæ, per quæ peccatores assumuntur a Deo. Et, in hac donatione, non habet locum personarum acceptio ; quia quilibet, absque injustitia, potest de suo dare quantum vult, et cui vult : secundum illud (Matt. xx.). Annon licet mihi quod volo facere? tolle quod tuum est et vade," i.e., " There is a twofold rendering or giving, the one a matter of justice, whereby that is paid to a man which was due to him. Here it is possible for us to act partially and with respect of persons." [Thus, for example's sake, if I owe money to two men, one of whom is rich, the other poor, and I pay the rich man because he has it in his power to sue me, but defraud the other because of his inability to do himself justice, I should be a respecter of persons. But as Aquinas goes on] : " There is a second kind of·rendering or giving, which is a branch of mere bounty and liberality, by which that is freely bestowed on any man which was not due to him : such are the gifts of grace whereby sinners are received of God. In the bestowment of grace respect of persons is absolutely out of the question, because everyone may, and can, without the least shadow of injustice, give as much of his own as he will and to whom he will, according to that passage in Matt. xx., ' Is it not lawful for me to do what I will [with my own]? take up that which is thine and go thy way.' "—Aquin. Summ. Theol. 2-2dæ Qu. 63, A. 1.

On the whole it is evident that respect of persons can only have place in matters of justice, and is but another name for perversion of justice, consequently it has nothing to do with matters of mere goodness and bounty, as all the blessings of grace and salvation are.

* Tom. 2, Epist. 105, ad Sixtum Presb.

so that the condemned sinner cannot allege that he is unworthy of his punishment, nor the saint vaunt or boast as if he was worthy of his reward. Thus, in the whole course of this procedure, there is no respect of persons. They who are condemned and they who are set at liberty constituted originally one and the same lump, equally infected with sin and liable to vengeance. Hence the justified may learn from the condemnation of the rest that that would have been their own punishment had not God's free grace stepped in to their rescue."

Before I conclude this head, I will obviate a fallacious objection very common in the mouths of our opponents. " How," they say, " is the doctrine of reprobation reconcilable with the doctrine of a future judgment? " To which I answer that there need be no pains to reconcile these two, since they are so far from interfering with each other that one follows from the other, and the former renders the latter absolutely necessary. Before the judgment of the great day, Christ does not so much act as the Judge of His creatures as their absolute Lord and Sovereign. From the first creation to the final consummation of all things He does, in consequence of His own eternal and immutable purpose (as a Divine Person), graciously work in and on His own elect, and permissively harden the reprobate. But when all the transactions of providence and grace are wound up in the last day, He will then properly sit as Judge, and openly publish and solemnly ratify, if I may so say, His everlasting decrees by receiving the elect, body and soul, into glory, and by passing sentence on the non-elect (not for their having done what they could not help, but) for their wilful ignorance of Divine things and their absolute unbelief, for their omissions of moral duty and for their repeated iniquities and transgressions.

POSITION 9.—Notwithstanding God's predestination is most certain and unalterable, so that no elect person can perish nor any reprobate be saved, yet it does not follow from thence that all precepts, reproofs and exhortations on the part of God, or prayers on the part of man, are useless, vain and insignificant.

(1) These are not useless with regard to the elect, for they are necessary means of bringing them to the knowledge of the truth at first, afterwards of stirring up their pure minds by way of remembrance, and of edifying and establishing them in faith, love and holiness. Hence that of St. Augustine :* '' The commandment will tell thee, O man, what thou oughtest to have, reproof will show thee wherein thou art wanting, and praying will teach thee from whom thou must receive the supplies which thou wantest.''

(2) Nor are these vain with regard to the reprobate, for precept, reproof and exhortation may, if duly attended to, be a means of making them careful to adjust their moral, external conduct according to the rules of decency, justice and regularity, and thereby prevent much inconvenience to themselves and injury to society. And as for prayer, it is the duty of all without exception. Every created being (whether elect or reprobate matters not as to this point) is, as such, dependent on the Creator for all things, and, if dependent, ought to have recourse to Him, both in a way of supplication and thanksgiving.

(3) But to come closer still. That absolute predestination does not set aside, nor render superfluous the use of preaching, exhortation, etc., we prove from the examples of Christ Himself and His apostles, who all taught and insisted upon the article of predestination, and yet took every opportunity of preaching to sinners and enforced their ministry with proper rebukes, invitations and exhortations as occasion required. Though they showed unanswerably that salvation is the free gift of God and lies entirely at His sovereign disposal, that men can of themselves do nothing spiritually good, and that it is God who of His own pleasure works in them

---

* De Corrept. et Grat., chap. 3.

both to will and to do, yet they did not neglect to address their auditors as beings possessed of reason and conscience, nor omitted to remind them of their duties as such; but showed them their sin and danger by nature, and laid before them the appointed way and method of salvation as exhibited in the Gospel.

Our Saviour Himself expressly, and *in terminis*, assures us that no man can come to Him except the Father draw him, and yet He says, "Come unto Me, all ye that labour," etc. St. Peter told the Jews that they had fulfilled "the determinate counsel and foreknowledge of God" in putting the Messiah to death (Acts ii.), and yet sharply rebukes them for it. St. Paul declares, "It is not of him that willeth nor of him that runneth," and yet exhorts the Corinthians so to run as to obtain the prize. He assures us that "we know not what to pray for as we ought" (Rom. viii.), and yet directs us to "pray without ceasing" (1 Thess. v.). He avers that the foundation or decree of the Lord standeth sure, and yet cautions him who "thinks he stands, to take heed lest he fall" (1 Tim. ii.). St. James, in like manner, says that "every good and perfect gift cometh down from above," and yet exhorts those who want wisdom to ask it of God. So, then, all these being means whereby the elect are frequently enlightened into the knowledge of Christ, and by which they are, after they have believed through grace, built up in Him, and are means of their perseverance in grace to the end; these are so far from being vain and insignificant that they are highly useful and necessary, and answer many valuable and important ends, without in the least shaking the doctrine of predestination in particular or the analogy of faith in general. Thus St. Augustine :* "We must preach, we must reprove, we must pray, because they to whom grace is given will hear and act accordingly, though they to whom grace is not given will do neither."

---

* De Bon. Persev., cap. 14.

CHAPTER V.

SHOWING THAT THE SCRIPTURE DOCTRINE OF PREDESTINA-
TION SHOULD BE OPENLY PREACHED AND INSISTED ON, AND
FOR WHAT REASONS.

UPON the whole, it is evident that the doctrine of God's
eternal and unchangeable predestination should neither
be wholly suppressed and laid aside, nor yet be confined
to the disquisition of the learned and speculative only;
but likewise should be publicly taught from the pulpit
and the press, that even the meanest of the people may
not be ignorant of a truth which reflects such glory on
God, and is the very foundation of happiness to man.
Let it, however, be preached with judgment and discretion, *i.e.*, delivered by the preacher as it is delivered in
Scripture, and no otherwise. By which means, it can
neither be abused to licentiousness nor misapprehended
to despair, but will eminently conduce to the knowledge,
establishment, improvement and comfort of them that
hear. That predestination ought to be preached, I thus
prove :—

I.—The Gospel is to be preached, and that not partially and by piece-meal, but the whole of it. The commission runs, "Go forth and preach *the Gospel*"; the
Gospel itself, even all the Gospel, without exception or
limitation. So far as the Gospel is maimed or any branch
of the evangelical system is suppressed and passed over
in silence, so far the Gospel is *not* preached. Besides,
there is scarce any other distinguishing doctrine of the
Gospel can be preached, in its purity and consistency,
without this of predestination. Election is the golden
thread that runs through the whole Christian system; it
is the leaven that pervades the whole lump. Cicero says
of the various parts of human learning : "*Omnes artes,
quæ ad humanitatem pertinent, habent quoddam com-
mune vinculum, et quasi cognatione quadam inter se
continentur,*" *i.e.*, The whole circle of arts have a kind
of mutual bond and connection, and by a sort of reciprocal

relationship are held together and interwoven with each other. Much the same may be said of this important doctrine : it is the bond which connects and keeps together the whole Christian system, which, without this, is like a system of sand, ever ready to fall to pieces. It is the cement which holds the fabric together ; nay, it is the very soul that animates the whole frame. It is so blended and interwoven with the entire scheme of Gospel doctrine that when the former is excluded, the latter bleeds to death. An ambassador is to deliver the whole message with which he is charged. He is to omit no part of it, but must declare the mind of the sovereign he represents, fully and without reserve. He is to say neither more or less than the instructions of his court require, else he comes under displeasure, perhaps loses his head. Let the ministers of Christ weigh this well.

Nor is the Gospel to be preached only, but preached to every creature, *i.e.*, to reasonable beings promiscuously and at large, to all who frequent the Christian ministry, of every state and condition in life, whether high or low, young or old, learned or illiterate. All who attend on the ministrations of Christ's ambassadors have a right to hear the Gospel fully, clearly and without mincing. Preach it, says Christ (Mark xvi. 15), κηρύξατε, publish it abroad, be its cryers and heralds, proclaim it aloud, tell it out, keep back no part of it, spare not, lift up your voices like trumpets. Now, a very considerable branch of this Gospel is the doctrine of God's eternal, free, absolute and irreversible election of some persons in Christ to everlasting life. The saints were singled out, in God's eternal purpose and choice, *ut crederent*, to be endued with faith, and thereby fitted for their destined salvation. By their interest in the gratuitous, unalienable love of the blessed Trinity they come to be, subjectively, saints and believers, so that their whole salvation, from the first plan of it in the Divine mind to the consummation of it in glory, is at once a matter of mere grace and of absolute certainty ; while they who die without faith and holiness prove thereby that they were not included in this elect number, and were not written in the book of life.

The justice of God's procedure herein is unquestionable. Out of a corrupt mass, wherein not one was better than another, He might (as was observed before) love and choose whom and as many as He pleased. It was likewise, without any shadow of injustice, at His option, whom and how many He would pass by. His not choosing them was the fruit of His sovereign will, but His condemning them, after death, and in the last day, is the fruit (not of their non-election, which was no fault of theirs, but) of their own positive transgressions. The elect, therefore, have the utmost reason to love and glorify God which any beings can possibly have, and the sense of what He has done for them is the strongest motive to obedience. On the other hand, the reprobates have nothing to complain of, since whatever God does is just and right, and so it will appear to be (however darkly matters may appear to us now) when we see Him as He is and know Him even as we are known.

And now why should not this doctrine be preached and insisted upon in public?—a doctrine which is of express revelation, a doctrine that makes wholly for the glory of God, which conduces, in a most peculiar manner, to the conversion, comfort and sanctification of the elect, and leaves even the ungodly themselves without excuse. But perhaps you may still be inclined to question whether predestination be indeed a Scripture doctrine. If so, let me by way of sample beg you to consider the following declarations—first, of Christ; secondly, of His apostles.

"If the mighty works that have been done in thee had been done in Tyre and Sidon, they would have repented," etc. (Matt. xi.), whence it is evident that the Tyrians and Sidonians, at least the majority of them, died in a state of impenitency, but that if God had given them the same means of grace afforded to Israel they would not have died impenitent, yet those means were

I

not granted them. How can this be accounted for? Only on the single principle of peremptory predestination flowing from the sovereign will of God. No wonder, then, that our Lord concludes that chapter with these remarkable words, " I thank Thee, O Father, Lord of heaven and earth, because Thou hast hid these things from the wise and prudent, and hast revealed them unto babes : even so, Father, for so it seemed good in Thy sight." Where Christ thanks the Father for doing that very thing which Arminians exclaim against as unjust and censure as partial.

" To you it is given to know the mysteries of the kingdom of heaven, but to them it is not given " (Matt. xiii.).

" To sit on My right hand and on My left is not Mine to give, αλλ οις ητοιμασαι ὑπο τοῦ πατρός μου, except to them for whom it hath been prepared by My Father," q.d., salvation is not a precarious thing ; the seats in glory were disposed of long ago in My Father's intention and destination ; I can only assign them to such persons as they were prepared for in His decree " (Matt. xx. 23).

" Many are called, but few chosen " (Matt. xxii), *i.e.*, all who live under the sound of the Gospel will not be saved, but those only who are elected unto life.

" For the elect's sake those days shall be shortened " (Matt. xxiv.), and ibid, " If it were possible, they should deceive the very elect," where, it is plain, Christ teaches two things : (1) that there is a certain number of persons who are elected to grace and glory, and (2) that it is absolutely impossible for these to be deceived into total or final apostacy.

" Come, ye blessed of My Father, inherit the kingdom prepared for you from the foundation of the world " (Matt. xxv.).

" Unto you it is given to know the mystery of the kingdom of God, but to them that are without " (*i.e.*, out of the pale of election) " all these things are done in parables ; that seeing, they may see, and not perceive :

and hearing, they may hear, and not understand : lest at any time, they should be converted, and their sins should be forgiven them '' (Mark xi.).

'' Rejoice, because your names are written in heaven '' (Luke x.).

'' It is your Father's good pleasure to give you the kingdom '' (Luke xii.).

'' One shall be taken and the other shall be left (Luke xvii.).

'' All that the Father hath given Me shall come unto Me '' (John vi.), as much as to say these shall but the rest cannot.

'' He that is of God, heareth God's words; ye therefore hear them not, because ye are not of God '' (John viii.), not chosen of Him.

'' Ye believe not, because ye are not of My sneep '' (John x.).

'' Ye have not chosen Me, but I have chosen you '' (John xv.).

I come now, second, to the Apostles.

'' They believed not on Him, that the saying of Esaias the prophet might be fulfilled which he spake ; Lord, who hath believed our report? and to whom hath the arm of the Lord been revealed?   Therefore they could not believe, because that Esaias said again, He hath blinded their eyes and hardened their heart, that they should not see with their eyes, nor understand with their heart, and be converted, and I should heal them '' (John xii. 37, 40). Without certain prescience there could be no prophecy, and without predestination no certain prescience.   Therefore, in order to the accomplishment of prophecy, prescience and predestination, we are expressly told that these persons could not believe ; οὐκ ἠδυναντο, they were not able, it was out of their power.   In short, there is hardly a page in St. John's Gospel which does not, either expressly or implicitly, make mention of election and reprobation.

St. Peter says of Judas, '' Men and brethren, the

Scriptures must needs have been fulfilled, which the Holy Ghost, by the mouth of David, spake before concerning Judas " (Acts i.). So, " That he might go to his own place " (ver. xxv.), to the place of punishment appointed for him.

" Him, being delivered by the determinate counsel and foreknowledge of God, ye have taken, and with wicked hands have crucified and slain " (Acts ii.).

" Herod, and Pontius Pilate, and the Gentiles, and the people of Israel, were gathered together, for to do whatsoever Thy hand and Thy counsel determined before to be done " (Acts iv.) : προωρισε γενεσθαι, predestinated should come to pass.

" And as many as were ordained to eternal life, believed " (Acts xiii.) : τεταγμένοι, designed, destined or appointed unto life.

Concerning the Apostle Paul, what shall I say? Everyone that has read his epistles knows that they teem with predestination from beginning to end.* I shall only give one or two passages, and begin with that famous chain : " whom He did foreknow " (or forelove, for to know often signifies in Scripture to love) " He also did predestinate to be conformed to the image of His Son, that he might be the firstborn among many brethren," that, as in all things else, so in the business of election Christ might have the pre-eminence, He being first chosen as a Saviour, and they in Him to be saved by Him : " moreover, whom He did predestinate, them He also called ; and whom He called, them He also justified ; and whom He justified, them He also glorified " (Rom. viii.).

---

*A friend of mine, who has a large property in Ireland, was conversing one day with a popish tenant of his upon religion. Among other points, they discussed the practice of having public prayers in an unknown tongue. My friend took down a New Testament from his book case and read part of 1 Cor. xiv. When he had finished, the poor zealous papist rose up from his chair and said with great vehemence, " I verily believe St. Paul was a heretic ! "

Can the person who carefully reads the epistles of that great apostle doubt of his having been a thorough-paced predestinarian?

Chapters ix., x. and xi. of the same epistle are professed dissertations on, and illustrations of the doctrine of God's decrees, and contain, likewise, a solution of the principal objections brought against that doctrine.

"Who separated me from my mother's womb and called me by His grace" (Gal. i.).

The first chapter of Ephesians treats of little else but election and predestination.

After observing that the reprobates perish wilfully, the apostle, by a striking transition, addresses himself to the elect Thessalonians, saying, "But we are bound to give thanks unto God always for you, brethren, beloved of the Lord, because God hath, from the beginning, chosen you to salvation, through sanctification of the Spirit and belief of the truth" (2 Thess. ii.).

"Who hath saved us and called us with an holy calling, not according to our works, but according to His own purpose, and grace, which was given us in Christ before the world began" (2 Tim. i.).

St. Jude, on the other hand, describes the reprobate as "ungodly men, who were, of old, foreordained to this condemnation."

Another apostle makes this peremptory declaration, "Who stumble at the word, being disobedient, whereunto also they were appointed: but ye are a chosen generation [γένος ἐκλεκτόν, an elect race], a royal priesthood, an holy nation, a peculiar people, λαὸς εἰς περιποίησιν, a people purchased to be His peculiar property and possession" (1 Peter ii. 8, 9); to all which may be added, "Whose names were not written in the book of life from the foundation of the world" (Rev. xvii. 8).

All these texts are but as an handful to the harvest, and yet are both numerous and weighty enough to decide the point with any who pay the least deference to Scripture authority. And let it be observed that Christ and His apostles delivered these matters, not to some privileged persons only, but to all at large who had ears to hear and eyes to read. Therefore, it is incumbent on every faithful minister to tread in their steps by doing likewise, nor is that minister a faithful one, faithful to Christ, to truth and to souls, who keeps back any part of the counsel of God, and buries those doctrines in silence which he is commanded to preach upon the house-tops.

The great St. Augustine, in his valuable treatise, *De Bono Persever.*, effectually obviates the objections of those who are burying the doctrine of predestination in silence. He shows that it ought to be publicly taught, describes the necessity and usefulness of preaching it, and points out the manner of doing it to edification. And since some persons have condemned St. Augustine, by bell, book and candle, for his stedfast attachment to and nervous, successful defences of the decrees of God, let us hear what Luther, that great light in the Church, thought respecting the argument before us.

Erasmus (in most other respects a very excellent man) affected to think that it was of dangerous consequence to propagate the doctrine of predestination either by preaching or writing. His words are these : '' What can be more useless than to publish this paradox to the world, namely, that whatever we do is done, not by virtue of our own free-will, but in a way of necessity, etc. ? What a wide gap does the publication of this tenet open among men for the commission of all ungodliness ! What wicked person will reform his life? Who will dare to believe himself a favourite of heaven? Who will fight against his own corrupt inclinations? Therefore, where is either the need or the utility of spreading these notions from whence so many evils seem to flow?.''

To which Luther replies : '' If, my Erasmus, you consider these paradoxes (as you term them) to be no more than the inventions of men, why are you so extravagantly heated on the occasion? In that case, your arguments affect not me, for there is no person now living in the world who is a more avowed enemy to the doctrines of men than myself. But if you believe the doctrines in debate between us to be (as indeed they are) the doctrines of God, you must have bid adieu to all sense of shame and decency thus to oppose them. I will not ask, ' Whither is the modesty of Erasmus fled? ' but, which is much more important, ' Where, alas! are your fear and reverence of the Deity when you roundly declare that this branch of truth which He has revealed from heaven, is, at best, useless and unnecessary to be known?' What! shall the glorious Creator be taught by you, His creature, what is fit to be preached and what to be suppressed? Is the adorable God so very defective in wisdom and prudence as not to know till you instruct Him what would be useful and what pernicious? Or could not He, whose understanding is infinite, foresee, previous to His revelation of this doctrine, what would be the consequences of His revealing it until those consequences were pointed out by you? You cannot, you dare not say this. If, then, it was the Divine pleasure to make known these things in His Word, and to bid His messengers publish them abroad, and leave the consequences of their so doing to the wisdom and providence of Him in whose name they speak, and whose message they declare, who art thou, O Erasmus, that thou shouldest reply against God and say to the Almighty, ' What doest Thou? '

" St. Paul, discoursing of God, declares peremptorily, ' Whom He will He hardeneth,' and again, ' God willing to show His wrath,' etc. And the apostle did not write this to have it stifled among a few persons and buried in a corner, but wrote it to the Christians at Rome, which was, in effect, bringing this doctrine upon the stage of the whole world, stamping an universal imprimatur upon it, and publishing it to believers at large throughout the earth. What can sound harsher in the uncircumcised ears of carnal men than those words of Christ, ' Many are called, but few chosen '? And elsewhere, ' I know whom I have chosen.' Now, these and similar assertions of Christ and His apostles are the very positions which you, O Erasmus, brand as useless and hurtful. You

object, ' If these things are so, who will endeavour to
amend his life? ' I answer, ' Without the Holy Ghost,
no man can amend his life to purpose ' Reformation is
but varnished hypocrisy unless it proceed from grace.
The elect and truly pious are amended by the Spirit of
God, and those of mankind who are not amended by Him
will perish.

" You ask, moreover, ' Who will dare to believe himself a favourite of heaven? ' I answer, ' It is not in
man's own power to believe himself such upon just
grounds until he is enabled from above.' But the elect
shall be so enabled; they shall believe themselves to be
what indeed they are. As for the rest who are not endued
with faith, they shall perish, raging and blaspheming as
you do now. ' But,' say you, ' these doctrines open a
door to ungodliness.' I answer, ' Whatever door they
may open to the impious and profane, yet they open a
door of righteousness to the elect and holy, and show
them the way to heaven and the path of access unto
God.' Yet you would have us abstain from the mention
of these grand doctrines, and leave our people in the dark
as to their election of God; the consequence of which
would be that every man would bolster himself up with
a delusive hope of share in that salvation which is supposed to lie open to all, and thus genuine humility and
the practical fear of God would be kicked out of doors.
This would be a pretty way indeed of stopping up the
gap Erasmus complains of! Instead of closing up the
door of licentiousness, as is falsely pretended, it would
be, in fact, opening a gulf into the nethermost hell.

" Still you urge, ' Where is either the necessity or
utility of preaching predestination? ' God Himself
teaches it or commands us to teach it, and that is answer
enough. We are not to arraign the Deity and bring the
motives of His will to the test of human scrutiny, but
simply to revere both Him and it. He, who alone is
all-wise and all-just, can in reality (however things appear
to us) do wrong to no man, neither can He do anything

unwisely or rashly. And this consideration will suffice to silence all the objections of truly religious persons. However, let us for argument's sake go a step farther. I will venture to assign over and above two very important reasons why these doctrines should be publicly taught :—

"(1) For the humiliation of our pride and the manifestation of Divine grace. God hath assuredly promised His favour to the truly humble. By truly humble, I mean those who are endued with repentance, and despair of saving themselves; for a man can never be said to be really penitent and humble until he is made to know that his salvation is not suspended in any measure whatever on his own strength, machinations, endeavours, free-will or works, but entirely depends on the free pleasure, purpose, determination and efficiency of another, even of God alone. Whilst a man is persuaded that he has it in his power to contribute anything, be it ever so little, to his own salvation, he remains in carnal confidence; he is not a self-despairer, and therefore he is not duly humbled before God; so far from it, that he hopes some favourable juncture or opportunity will offer when he may be able to lend a helping hand to the business of his salvation. On the contrary, whoever is truly convinced that the whole work depends singly and absolutely on the will of God, who alone is the author and finisher of salvation, such a person despairs of all self-assistance, he renounces his own will and his own strength, he waits and prays for the operation of God, nor waits and prays in vain. For the elect's sake, therefore, these doctrines are to be preached, that the chosen of God, being humbled by the knowledge of His truths, self-emptied and sunk, as it were, into nothing in His presence, may be saved in Christ with eternal glory. This, then, is one inducement to the publication of the doctrine, that the penitent may be made acquainted with the promise of grace, plead it in prayer to God, and receive it as their own.

"(2) The nature of the Christian faith requires it.

Faith has to do with things not seen. And this is one of the highest degrees of faith, stedfastly to believe that God is infinitely merciful, though He saves, comparatively, but few and condemns so many, and that He is strictly just, though of His own will He makes such numbers of mankind necessarily liable to damnation. Now, these are some of the unseen things whereof faith is the evidence, whereas, was it in my power to comprehend them or clearly to make out how God is both inviolably just and infinitely merciful, notwithstanding the display of wrath and seeming inequality in His dispensations respecting the reprobate, faith would have little or nothing to do. But now, since these matters cannot be adequately comprehended by us in the present state of imperfection, there is room for the exercise of faith. The truths therefore, respecting predestination in all its branches, should be taught and published, they, no less than the other mysteries of Christian doctrine, being proper objects of faith on the part of God's people.''*

With Luther the excellent Bucer agrees, particularly on Eph. i., where his words are : '' There are some who affirm that election is not to be mentioned publicly to the people. But they judge wrongly. The blessings which God bestows on man are not to be suppressed, but insisted and enlarged upon, and, if so, surely the blessing of predestination unto life, which is the greatest blessing of all, should not be passed over.'' And a little after he adds : '' Take away the remembrance and consideration of our election, and then, good God ! what weapons have we left us wherewith to resist the temptations of Satan? As often as he assaults our faith (which he is frequently doing) we must constantly and without delay have recourse to our election in Christ as to a city of refuge. Meditation upon the Father's appointment of us to eternal life is the best antidote against the evil surmisings

---

* Lutherus, De Serv. Arbitr. in respons. ad ult. part. præfat. Erasmi.

of doubtfulness and remaining unbelief. If we are entirely void of all hope and assurance, respecting our
interest in this capital privilege, what solid and comfortable expectation can we entertain of future blessedness?
How can we look upon God as our gracious Father and
upon Christ as our unchangeable Redeemer? without
which I see not how we can ever truly love God; and if
we have no true love towards Him, how can we yield
acceptable obedience to Him?   Therefore, those persons
are not to be heard who would have the doctrine of election laid (as it were) asleep, and seldom or never make its
appearance in the congregations of the faithful.''

To what these great men have so nervously advanced
permit me to add, that the doctrine of predestination is
not only useful, but absolutely necessary to be taught
and known.

(1) For without it we cannot form just and becoming
ideas of God.   Thus, unless He certainly foreknows and
foreknew from everlasting all things that should come to
pass, His understanding would not be infinite, and a
Deity of limited understanding is no Deity at all.   Again,
we cannot suppose Him to have foreknown anything
which He had not previously decreed, without setting up
a series of causes, *extra Deum*, and making the Deity
dependent for a great part of the knowledge He has upon
the will and works of His creatures, and upon a combination of circumstances exterior to Himself.   Therefore, His determinate plan, counsel and purpose (*i.e.*,
His own predestination of causes and effects) is the only
basis of His foreknowledge, which foreknowledge could
neither be certain nor independent but as founded on
His own antecedent decree.

(2) He alone is entitled to the name of true God who
governs all things, and without whose will (either efficient
or permissive) nothing is or can be done.   And such is
the God of the Scriptures, against whose will not a
sparrow can die nor an hair fall from our heads (Matt. x.)
Now what is predestination but the determining *will* of

God? I defy the subtlest semi-pelagian in the world to form or convey a just and worthy notion of the Supreme Being without admitting Him to be the great cause of all causes else, Himself dependent on none, who willed from eternity how He would act in time, and settled a regular, determinate scheme of what He would do and permit to be done from the beginning to the consummation of the world. A contrary view of the Deity is as inconsistent with reason itself, and with the very religion of nature, as it is with the decisions of revelation.

(3) Nor can we rationally conceive of an independent, all-perfect first cause without allowing Him to be unchangeable in His purposes. His decrees and His essence coincide, consequently a change in those would infer an alteration in this. Nor can that being be the true God whose will is variable, fluctuating and indeterminate, for His will is Himself willing. A Deity without decrees and decrees without immutability are, of all inventions that ever entered the heart of man, the most absurd.

(4) Without predestination to plan, and without providence to put that plan in execution, what becomes of God's omnipotence? It vanishes into air. It becomes a mere nonentity. For what sort of omnipotence is that which may be baffled and defeated by the very creatures it has made? Very different is the idea of this attribute suggested by the Psalmist, " Whatsoever the Lord willed, that did He, in heaven and in earth, in the sea and in all deep places " (Psalm cxiii.), *i.e.*, He not only made them when He would, but orders them when made.

(5) He alone is the true God, according to Scripture representation, who saves by His mere mercy and voluntary grace those whom He hath chosen, and righteously condemns (for their sins) those whom He thought fit to pass by. But without predestination there could be no such thing either as sovereign mercy or voluntary grace. For, after all, what is predestination but His decree to save some of His mere goodness, and to condemn others in His just judgment? Now it is most evident that the

Scripture doctrine of *pre-determination* is the clearest mirror wherein to see and contemplate these essential attributes of God.   Here they all shine forth in their fulness of harmony and lustre.   Deny predestination and you deny (though, perhaps, not intentionally, yet by necessary consequence) the adorable perfections of the Godhead : in concealing that, you throw a veil over these ; and in preaching that, you hold up these to the comfort, the establishment and the admiration of the believing world.

II.—Predestination is to be preached because the *grace* of God (which stands opposed to all human worthiness) cannot be maintained without it.   The excellent St. Augustine makes use of this very argument.   " If," says he, " these two privileges (namely, faith itself and final perseverance in faith) are the gifts of God, and if God foreknew on whom He would bestow these gifts (and who can doubt of so evident a truth?), it is necessary for predestination to be preached as the sure and invincible bulwark of that true grace of God, which is given to men without any consideration of merit."* Thus argued St. Augustine against the Pelagians, who taught that grace is offered to all men alike ; that God, for His part, equally wills the salvation of all, and that it is in the power of man's free-will to accept or reject the grace and salvation so offered.   Which string of errors do, as Augustine justly observes, centre in this grand point, *gratiam secundum nostra merita dari* : that God's grace is not free, but the fruit of man's desert.

Now the doctrine of predestination batters down this delusive Babel of free-will and merit.   It teaches us that, if we do indeed will and desire to lay hold on Christ and salvation by Him, this will and desire are the effect of God's secret purpose and effectual operation, for *He* it is who worketh in us both to will and to do of His own good pleasure, that he that glorieth should glory in the

---

* De Bono Persever. cap. 21.

Lord. There neither is nor can be any medium between predestinating grace and salvation by human merit. We must believe and preach one or the other, for they can never stand together. No attempts to mingle and reconcile these two incompatible opposites can ever succeed, the apostle himself being judge. '' If (says he) it (namely, election) be by grace, then is it no more of works, otherwise grace is no more grace : but, if it be of works, then is it no more grace ; otherwise work is no more work '' (Rom xi. 6). Exactly agreeable to which is that of St. Augustine : '' Either predestination is to be preached as expressly as the Scriptures deliver it, namely, that with regard to those whom He hath chosen, ' the gifts and calling of God are without repentance,' or we must roundly declare, as the Pelagians do, that grace is given according to merit.''* Most certain it is that the doctrine of gratuitous justification *through* Christ can only be supported on that of our gratuitous predestination *in* Christ, since the latter is the cause and foundation of the former.

III.—By the preaching of predestination man is duly humbled, and God alone is exalted ; human pride is levelled, and the Divine glory shines untarnished because unrivalled. This the sacred writers positively declare. Let St. Paul be spokesman for the rest, "*Having predestinated us—to the praise of the glory of His grace*" (Eph. i. 5, 6). But how is it possible for us to render unto God the praises due to the glory of His grace without laying this threefold foundation?

(1) That whosoever are or shall be saved are saved by His alone grace in Christ in consequence of His eternal purpose passed before they had done any one good thing.

(2) That what good thing soever is begun to be wrought in our souls (whether it be illumination of the understanding, rectitude of will or purity of affections) was begun altogether of God alone, by whose invincible agency grace is at first conferred, afterwards maintained, and finally crowned.

---

* De Bono Persever. cap. 16.

(3) That the work of internal salvation (the sweet and certain prelude to eternal glory) was not only begun in us of His mere grace alone, but that its continuance, its progress and increase are no less free and totally unmerited than its first original donation. Grace alone makes the elect gracious, grace alone keeps them gracious, and the same grace alone will render them everlastingly glorious in the heaven of heavens.

Conversion and salvation must, in the very nature of things, be wrought and effected either by ourselves alone, or by ourselves and God together, or *solely by God Himself.* The Pelagians were for the first. The Arminians are for the second. True believers are for the last, because the last hypothesis, and that only, is built on the strongest evidence of Scripture, reason and experience : it most effectually hides pride from man, and sets the crown of undivided praise upon the head, or rather casts it at the feet, of that glorious *Triune God*, who worketh all in all. But this is a crown which no sinners ever yet cast before the throne of God who were not first led into the transporting views of His gracious decree to save, freely and of His own will, the people of His eternal love. Exclude, therefore, O Christian, the article of *sovereign predestination* from thy ministry or from thy faith, and acquit thyself if thou art able from the charge of robbing God.

When God does, by the omnipotent exertion of His Spirit, effectually call any of mankind in time to the actual knowledge of Himself in Christ; when He, likewise, goes on to sanctify the sinners He has called, making them to excel in all good works, and to persevere in the love and resemblance of God to their lives' end, the observing part of the unawakened world may be apt to conclude that these converted persons might receive such measures of grace from God because of some previous qualifications, good dispositions, or pious desires and internal preparations, discovered in them by the all-seeing eye, which, if true, would indeed transfer the praise from the

Creator and consign it to the creature. But the doctrine
of *predestination*, absolute, free, unconditional *predestination*, here steps in and gives God His own. It lays
the axe to the root of human boasting, and cuts down
(for which reason the natural man hates it) every legal,
every independent, every self-righteous imagination that
would exalt itself against the grace of God and the glory
of Christ. It tells us that God hath blessed us with all
spiritual blessings in His Son, "according as He hath
chosen us in *Him* before the foundation of the world,"
in order to our being afterwards made "holy and blame-
less before Him in love" (Eph. i.).

Of course, whatever truly and spiritually good thing
is found in any person, it is the especial gift and work
of God, given and wrought in consequence of eternal
unmerited election to grace and glory. Whence the
greatest saint cannot triumph over the most abandoned
sinner, but is led to refer the entire praise of his salvation, both from sin and hell, to the mere goodwill and
sovereign purpose of God, who hath graciously made him
to differ from that world which lieth in wickedness. Such
being the tendency of this blessed doctrine, how injurious
both to God and man would the suppression of it be !
Well does St. Augustine argue : "As the duties of *piety*
ought to be preached up, that he who hath ears to hear
may be instructed how to worship God aright ; and as
chastity should be publicly recommended and enforced,
that he who hath ears to hear may know how to possess
himself in sanctification ; and as *charity*, moreover, should
be inculcated from the pulpit, that he who hath ears to
hear may be excited to the ardent love of God and his
neighbour, in like manner should God's *predestination*
of His favours be openly preached, that he who hath ears
to .hear may learn to glory not in himself, but *in the
Lord*."*

IV.—Predestination should be publicly taught and

---

* De Bono Persever. cap. 20.

insisted upon, in order to confirm and strengthen true believers in the certainty and confidence of their salvation.* For when regenerate persons are told, and are enabled to believe, that the glorification of the elect is so assuredly fixed in God's eternal purpose that it is impossible for any of them to perish, and when the regenerate are led to consider themselves as actually belonging to this elect body of Christ, what can establish, strengthen and settle their faith like this? Nor is such a faith presumptuous, for every converted man may and ought to conclude himself elected, since God the Spirit *renews* those only who were *chosen* by God the Father and *redeemed* by God the Son. This is a "hope which maketh not ashamed," nor can possibly issue in disappointment if entertained by those into whose hearts the love of God is poured forth by the Holy Ghost given unto them (Rom. v. 5).

The holy triumph and assurance resulting from this blessed view are expressly warranted by the apostle, where he deduces effectual calling from a prior predestination, and infers the certainty of final salvation from effectual calling : "Whom He did *predestinate*, them He also *called;* and whom He called, them He also *justified;* and whom He justified, them He also *glorified*" (Rom. viii.). How naturally from such premises does the apostle add, "Who shall lay anything to the charge of God's elect?" Who and where is he that condemneth them? Who and what "shall separate us from the love of Christ? In all these things we are," and shall be, "more than conquerors through *Him* that hath loved us, for I am persuaded [πεπεισμαι,† I am MOST clearly and assuredly confident] that neither death, nor life, nor angels, nor

---

* Our venerable Reformers, in the 17th of our XXXIX. Articles, make the very same observation, and nearly in the same words : " The godly consideration of predestination and our election in Christ is full of sweet, pleasant and unspeakable comfort to godly persons, because it doth greatly *establish and confirm their faith of everlasting salvation* to be enjoyed through Christ," etc.

† *Certus sum*, Ar. Montan. *Certa fide persuasum mihi habeo*, Erasm. *Victa omni dubitatione*, Bengel. " I am assured," Dutch version.

principalities, nor powers, nor things present, nor things to come, nor height nor depth, nor any other creature shall be able to separate us from the love of God, which is in Christ Jesus our Lord." So elsewhere the foundation of the Lord, *i.e.*, His decree or purpose, according to election, " standeth sure, having this seal, *the Lord knoweth them that are His*," which is particularly noted by the apostle, lest true believers might be discouraged and begin to doubt of their own certain perseverance to salvation, either from a sense of their remaining imperfections or from observing the open apostacy of unregenerate professors (2 Tim. ii.). How little obliged, therefore, are the flock of Christ to those persons who would, by stifling the mention of predestination, expunge the sense and certainty of everlasting blessedness from the list of Christian privileges!

V.—Without the doctrine of predestination we cannot enjoy a lively sight and experience of God's special love and mercy towards us in Christ Jesus. Blessings, not peculiar, but conferred indiscriminately on every man, without distinction or exception, would neither be a proof of peculiar love in the donor nor calculated to excite peculiar wonder and gratitude in the receiver. For instance, rain from heaven, though an invaluable benefit, is not considered as an argument of God's special favour to some individuals above others : and why? because it falls on all alike, as much on the rude wilderness and the barren rock as on the cultivated garden and the fruitful field. But the blessing of election, somewhat like the Sibylline books, rises in value, proportionably to the fewness of its objects. So that, when we recollect that in the view of God (to whom all things are at once present) the whole mass of mankind was considered as justly liable to condemnation on account of original and actual iniquity, His selecting some individuals from among the rest and graciously setting them apart in Christ for salvation both from sin and punishment, were such acts of sovereign goodness as exhibit the exceeding greatness and the entire freeness of His love in the most awful, amiable and humbling light.

In order, then, that the special grace of God may shine, *predestination* must be preached, even the eternal and immutable predestination of His people to faith and everlasting life. "From those who are left under the power of guilt," says Augustine, "the person who is delivered from it may learn what he too must have suffered had not *grace* stepped in to his relief. And if it was that grace that interposed, it could not be the reward of man's merit, but the free gift of God's gratuitous goodness. Some, however, call it unjust for one to be delivered while another, though no more guilty than the former, is condemned ; if it be just to punish one, it would be but justice to punish both. I grant that both might have been justly punished. Let us therefore give thanks unto God our Saviour for not inflicting that vengeance on us, which, from the condemnation of our fellow-sinners, we may conclude to have been our desert, no less than theirs. Had they as well as we been ransomed from their captivity, we could have framed but little conception of the penal wrath due, in strictness of justice, to sin ; and, on the other hand, had none of the fallen race been ransomed and set at liberty, how could *Divine grace* have displayed the riches of its liberality ?"* The same evangelical father delivers himself elsewhere to the same effect. "Hence," says he, "appears the greatness of that grace by which so many are freed from condemnation, and they may form some idea of the misery, due to themselves, from the dreadfulness of the punishment that awaits the rest. Whence those who rejoice are taught to rejoice not in their own merits (*quæ paria esse vident damnatis*, for they see that *they have no more merit than the damned*), but in the Lord."†

VI.—Hence results another reason nearly connected with the former for the unreserved publication of this

---

* Epist. 105, ad Sixt. Presb. † De Predest. Sanctor, lib. 1, cap. 9.

doctrine, namely, that, from a sense of God's peculiar, eternal and unalterable love to His people, their hearts may be inflamed to love Him in return. Slender indeed will be my motives to the love of God on the supposition that my love to Him is beforehand with His to me, and that the very continuance of His favour is suspended on the weathercock of my variable will or the flimsy thread of my imperfect affection. Such a precarious, dependent love were unworthy of God, and calculated to produce but a scanty and cold reciprocation of love from man. At the happiest of times, and in the best of frames below, our love to God is but a spark (though small and quivering, yet inestimably precious, because Divinely kindled, fanned and maintained in the soul, and an earnest of better to come), whereas love, as it glows in God, is an immense *sun*, which shone without beginning, and shall shine without end. Is it probable, then, that the spark of human love should give being to the sun of divine, and that the lustre and warmth of this should depend on the glimmering of that? Yet so it must be if *predestination* is not true, and so it must be represented if predestination is not taught. Would you, therefore, know what it is to love God as your Father, Friend, and Saviour, you must fall down before His *electing mercy*. Until then you are only hovering about in quest of true felicity. But you will never find the door, much less can you enter into rest, until you are enabled to "love *Him because* He hath *first* loved you" (1 John iv. 19).

This being the case, it is evident that, without taking predestination into the account, genuine *morality* and the performance of truly *good works* will suffer, starve and die away. Love to God is the very fuel of acceptable obedience. Withdraw the fuel, and the flame expires. But the fuel of holy affection (if Scripture, experience and observation are allowed to carry any conviction) can only be cherished, maintained and increased in the heart by the sense and apprehension of God's predestinating love to us in Christ Jesus. Now, our obedience to God will always hold proportion to our love. If the one be relaxed and feeble, the other cannot be alert and vigorous, and, electing goodness being the very life and soul of the former, the latter, even *good works,* must flourish or decline in proportion as *election* is glorified or obscured.

VII.—Hence arises a seventh argument for the preaching of predestination, namely, that by it we may be excited to the practice of universal godliness. The knowledge of God's love to you will make you an ardent lover of God, and the more love you have to God, the more will you excel in all the duties and offices of love. Add to this that the Scripture view of predestination includes the means as well as the end. Christian pre-destinarians are for keeping together what God hath joined. He who is for attaining the end without going to it through the means is a self-deluding enthusiast. He, on the other hand, who carefully and conscientiously uses the means of salvation as steps to the end is the true Calvinist.

Now, eternal life being that to which the elect are ultimately destined, faith (the effect of saving grace) and sanctification (the effect of faith) are blessings to which the elect are intermediately appointed. "According as He hath chosen us in Him, before the foundation of the world, that we should be *holy* and without blame before Him in love" (Eph. i. 4). "We are His workmanship, created in Christ Jesus unto *good works,* which God hath before ordained that we should walk in them" (Eph. ii. 10). "Knowing, brethren beloved, your election of God . . . and ye became followers of us and of the Lord" (1 Thess. i. 4, 6). "God hath chosen you to salvation *through sanctification* of the Spirit and belief of the truth" (2 Thess. ii. 13). "Elect, according to the fore-knowledge [or ancient love] of God the Father through sanctification of the Spirit unto *obedience*" (1 Peter i. 2). Nor is salvation (the appointed end of election) at all the less secure in itself (but the more so) for standing neces-sarily connected with the intervening means, seeing both these and that are inseparably joined, in order to the certain accomplishment of that through these. It only demonstrates that without regeneration of the heart and purity of life, the elect themselves are not led to heaven. But, then, it is incontestible from the whole current of Scripture that these intermediate blessings shall most infallibly be vouchsafed to every elect person, in virtue of God's absolute covenant and through the effectual agency of His Almighty Spirit. Internal sanctification constitutes our meetness for the kingdom to which we were predestinated, and a course of external righteousness is one of the grand evidences by which we make our election sure to our own present comfort and apprehension of it.*

VIII.—Unless predestination be preached, we shall want one great inducement to the exercise of brotherly kindness and charity. When a converted person is assured, on one hand, that *all* whom God hath predestinated to eternal life shall infallibly enjoy that eternal life to which they are chosen, and, on the other hand, when he discerns the signs of election, not only in himself, but also in the rest of his fellow-believers, and concludes from thence (as in a judgment of charity he ought) that they are as really elected as himself, how must his heart glow with love to his Christian brethren! How feelingly will he sympathise with them in their distresses! How tenderly will he bear with their infirmities! How readily will he relieve the former, and how easily overlook the latter! Nothing will so effectually knit together the hearts of God's people in time as the belief of their having been written by name in one book of life from ever-

---

* 2 Peter i. 10, Give diligence to make your calling and election, βεβαίαν, undoubted; *i.e.*, to get some solid and incontestible evidence of your predestination to life. βέβαιος *is de quo fiducia concipitur; is de quo nobis aliquid certo persuademus.*—Unde apud Thuc. 3. βέβαιος ειμι, τουτο ποιήσειν *certa fides habetur mihi, hoc facturum me esse.* Βεβαίως, *certo explorato.* Βεβαιουμαι, *fidem facio; pro comperto habeo.*" Scap—So, ελπις βεβαια is an undoubting hope (2 Cor. i. 7), and Βεβαιότερος λόγος is a more assured and unquestionable word of prophecy (2 Peter i. 19).

lasting, and the unshaken confidence of their future exaltation to one and the same state of glory above will occasion the strongest cement of affection below.

This was, possibly, one end of our Saviour's so frequently reminding His apostles of their election, namely, that from the sense of such an unspeakable blessing, in which they were all equally interested, they might learn to love one another with pure hearts fervently, and cultivate on earth that holy friendship which they well knew, from the immutability of God's decrees, would be eternally matured to the highest perfection and refinement in heaven. St. Paul, likewise, might have some respect to the same amiable inference when treating of the saints collectively, for he uses those sweet and endearing expressions, "He hath chosen *us*," "He hath predestinated *us*," etc., that believers, considering themselves as συνεκλεκτοι or co-elect in Christ, might be led to love each other with peculiar intenseness as the spiritual children of one electing Father, brethren in grace and joint-heirs of glory. Did the regenerate of the present age but practically advert to the everlasting nearness in which they stand related to each other, how happy would be the effect!

Hence it appears that, since the preaching of predestination is thus evidently calculated to kindle and keep alive the twofold congenial flame of love to God and love to man, it must, by necessary consequence, conduce to the advancement of universal obedience and to the performance of every social and religious duty,* which alone,

---

* Our excellent Bishop Davenant instances particularly in the great religious duty of prayer. "The consideration of election," says this learned and evangelical prelate, " doth stir up the faithful to constancy in prayer, for, having learnt that all good tending to salvation is prepared for them out of God's good pleasure, they are hereby encouraged to call for, and as it were to draw down from heaven by their prayers, those good things which, from eternity, were ordained for the elect. Moreover, the same Spirit of adoption, who beareth witness to our spirit, that we are God's chosen children, is also the Spirit of prayer and supplication, and enflameth our hearts to call daily upon our heavenly Father. Those, therefore, who from the certainty of predestination do pretend that the duty of prayer is superfluous, do plainly show that they

was there nothing else to recommend it, would be a sufficient motive to the public delivery of that important doctrine.

IX.—Lastly, without a due sense of predestination, we shall want the surest and the most powerful inducement to patience, resignation and dependence on God under every spiritual and temporal affliction.

How sweet must the following considerations be to a distressed believer! (1) There most certainly exists an almighty, all-wise and infinitely gracious God. (2) He has given me in times past, and is giving me at present (if I had but eyes to see it), many and signal intimations of His love to me, both in a way of providence and grace. (3) This love of His is immutable ; He never repents of it nor withdraws it. (4) Whatever comes to pass in time is the result of His will from everlasting, consequently (5) my afflictions were a part of His original plan, and are all ordered in number, weight and measure. (6) The very hairs of my head are (every one) counted by Him, nor can a single hair fall to the ground but in consequence of His determination. Hence (7) my distresses are not the result of chance, accident or a fortuitous combination of circumstances, but (8) the providential accomplishment of God's purpose, and (9) designed to answer some wise and gracious ends, nor (10) shall my affliction continue a moment longer than God sees meet. (11) He who brought me to it has promised to support me under it and to carry me through it. (12) All shall, most assuredly, work together for His glory and my good, therefore (13) " The cup which my heavenly Father hath given me to

---

are so far from having any certainty of their predestination that they have not the least sense thereof. To be slack and sluggish in prayer is not the property of those who, by the testimony of God's Spirit, have got assurance of their election, but rather of such as have either none or very small apprehension thereof. For as soon as anyone by believing doth conceive himself to be one of God's elect children, he earnestly desireth to procure unto himself by-prayer those good things which he believeth that God prepared for His children before the foundation of the world."—Bp. Davenant's Aniamadversions on an Arminian treatise, entitled " God's Love to Mankind," p. 526, and seq.

drink, shall I not drink it?" Yes, I will, in the strength He imparts, even rejoice in tribulation; and using the means of possible redress, which He hath or may hereafter put into my hands, I will commit myself and the event to Him, whose purpose cannot be overthrown, whose plan cannot be disconcerted, and who, whether I am resigned or not, will still *go on to work all things after the counsel of His own will.**

---

* The learned Lipsius thus writes to an unmarried friend, who appears to have referred himself to his judgment and direction : "*Sive uxor ducitur, sive omittitur, etc.* Whether you marry or live single, you will still have something or other to molest you, nor does the whole course of man's present sublunary life afford him a single draught of joy without a mixture of wormwood in the cup. This is the universal and immutable law, which to resist were no less vain than sinful and rebellious. As the wrestlers of old had their respective antagonists assigned them, not by their own choice, but by necessary lot, in like manner each of the human race has his peculiar destiny allotted to him by Providence. To conquer this is to endure it. All our strength in this warfare is to undergo the inevitable pressure. It is victory to yield ourselves to fate."—Lips. Epist. miscell. cent. 1, ep. 43, oper tom., 2, p. 54, Edit. Vesaliens, 1675

About two years after, this celebrated Christian Seneca wrote as follows to the same person (Theodore Leewius), who had married and just lost his wife in child-bed : "*Jam fatum quid? Æterna, ab æterno, in æternum, Dei lex:* What is fate? God's everlasting ordinance—an ordinance settled in eternity and for eternity, an ordinance which He can never repeal, disannul or set aside, either in whole or in part. Now, if this His decree be eternal, *a retro*, and immovable, *quoad futurum*, why does foolish man struggle and fight against that which must be? Especially, seeing fate is thus the offspring of God, why does impious man murmur and complain? You cannot justly find fault with anything determined or done by Him, as though it were evil or severe, for He is all goodness and benevolence. Were you to define His nature, you could not do it more suitably than in those terms. Is, therefore, your wife dead? *Debuit:* it is right she should be so. But was it right that she should die, and at that very time, and by that very kind of death? Most certainly. *Lex ita lata:* the decree so ordained it. The restless acumen of the human mind may sift and canvass the appointments of fate, but cannot alter them. Were we truly wise, we should be implicitly submissive, and endure with willingness what we must endure, whether we be willing or not. A due sense of our inability to reverse the disposals of Providence, and the consequent vanity of resisting them, would administer solid repose to our minds, and sheathe, if not remove, the anguish of affliction. And why should we even wish to resist? Fate's supreme ordainer is not only the all-wise God, but an all-gracious Father. Embrace every event as good and prosperous, though it may, for the present, carry an aspect of the reverse. Think you not that He

Above all, when the suffering Christian takes his election into the account, and knows that he was by an eternal and immutable act of God appointed to obtain salvation through our Lord Jesus Christ; that, of course, he hath a city prepared for him above, a building of God, a house not made with hands, but eternal in the heavens; and that the heaviest sufferings of the present life are not worthy to be compared with the glory which shall be revealed in the saints, what adversity can possibly befall us which the assured hope of blessings like these will not infinitely overbalance?

> " A comfort so divine,
> May trials well endure."

However keenly afflictions might wound us on their first access, yet, under the impression of such animating views, we should quickly come to ourselves again, and the arrows of tribulation would, in great measure, become pointless. Christians want nothing but absolute resignation to render them perfectly happy in every possible circumstance, and absolute resignation can only flow from an absolute belief of, and an absolute acquiescence in, God's absolute providence, founded on absolute predestination. The apostle himself draws these conclusions to our hand in Rom. viii., where, after having laid down, as most undoubted axioms, the eternity and immutability of God's purposes, he thus winds up the whole : " What shall we then say to these things? If God be for us, who can be against us? Who shall separate us from the love of Christ? Shall tribulation, or distress, or persecution, or famine, or nakedness, or peril, or sword? Nay, in all these things we are more than conquerors through Him that loved us."

Such, therefore, among others, being the *uses* that arise from the faithful preaching and the cordial reception

---

loves and careth for us more and better than we for ourselves? But as the tenderest parent below doth oftentimes cross the inclinations of his children, with a view to do them good, and obliges them both to do and to undergo many things against the bent of their wills, so does the great Parent of all."—Ibid, epist. 61, p. 82.

of predestination, may we not venture to affirm, with
Luther, *hac ignorata doctrina, neque fidem, neque ullum
Dei cultum, consistere posse?* that " our faith and all
right worship of God, depend in no small degree upon
our knowledge of that doctrine "?*

The excellent Melancthon, in his first Common Places
(which received the sanction of Luther's express approbation), does, in the first chapter, which treats professedly
of free-will and predestination, set out with clearing and
establishing the doctrine of God's decrees, and then proceeds to point out the necessity and manifold usefulness
of asserting and believing it. He even goes so far as to
affirm roundly that " a right fear of God and a true
confidence in Him can be learned more assuredly from
no other source than from the doctrine of predestination."
But Melancthon's judgment of these matters will best
appear from the whole passage, which the reader will find
in the book and chapter just referred to.

"*Divina predestinatio,*" says he, "*Libertatem homini
adimit*"; Divine predestination quite strips man of his
boasted liberty, for all things come to pass according to
God's fore-appointment, even the internal thoughts of all
creatures, no less than the external works. Therefore
the apostle gives us to understand that God " performeth
all things according to the counsel of His own will "
(Eph. i.), and our Lord Himself asks, "Are not two
sparrows sold for a farthing? yet one of them falleth not
to the ground without your Father " (Matt. x.). Pray
what can be more full to the point than such a declaration? So Solomon, " The Lord hath made all things for
Himself; yea, even the wicked for the day of evil "
(Prov. xvi.), and in chap. xx., " Man's goings are of the
Lord : how then can a man understand his own way? "
To which the prophet Jeremiah does also set his seal,
saying (chapter x.), " O Lord, I know that the way of
man is not in himself ; it is not in man that walketh to
direct his steps." The historical part of Scripture

---

* De Serv. Arbitr., cap. 20.

teaches us the same great truth. So (Gen. xv.) we read
that the iniquity of the Amorites was not yet full. In
1 Sam. ii. we are told that Eli's sons hearkened not to
his reproof, because the Lord would slay them. What
could bear a stronger resemblance to chance and accident
than Saul's calling upon Samuel, only with a view to
seek out his father's asses? (1 Sam. ix.). Yet the visit
was fore-ordained of God, and designed to answer a purpose little thought of by Saul (1 Sam. ix. 15, 16). See
also a most remarkable chain of predestinated events in
reference to Saul, and foretold by the prophet (1 Sam.
x. 2, 8).

In pursuance of the Divine pre-ordination, there went
with Saul a band of men, whose hearts God had touched
(1 Sam. x. 26). The harshness of king Rehoboam's
answer to the ten tribes, and the subsequent revolt of
those tribes from his dominion, are by the sacred historian
expressly ascribed to God's decree : " Wherefore the king
hearkened not unto the people ; for the cause was from
the Lord, that He might perform His saying, which the
Lord spake by Abijah the Shilonite unto Jeroboam the
son of Nebat " (1 Kings xii. 15). What is the drift of
the Apostle Paul (Rom. ix. and xi.), *quam ut omnia,
quæ fiunt, in destinationem divinam referat,* but to resolve all things that come to pass into God's destination?
The judgment of the flesh, or of mere unregenerate
reason, usually starts back from this truth with horror ;
but, on the contrary, the judgment of a spiritual man will
embrace it with affection. *Neque enim vel timorem Dei,
vel fiduciam in Deum, certius aliunde disces, quam ubi
imbueris animum hac de predestinatione sententia :* you
will not learn either the fear of God or affiance in Him
from a surer source than from getting your mind deeply
tinctured and seasoned with this doctrine of predestination.

Does not Solomon, in the Book of Proverbs, inculcate
it throughout, and justly, for how else could he direct
men to fear God and trust in Him? The same he does

in the Book of Ecclesiastes, nor had anything so powerful a tendency to repress the pride of man's encroaching reason, and to lower the swelling conceit of his supposed discretion, as the firm belief, *quod a Deo fiunt omnia,* that all things are from God. What invincible comfort did Christ impart to His disciples in assuring them that their very hairs were all numbered by the Creator? Is there, then (may an objector say), no such thing as contingency, no such thing as chance or fortune? No. *Omnia necessario evenire scripturæ docent;* the doctrine of Scripture is, that all things come to pass necessarily. Be it so that to you some events seem to happen contingently, you nevertheless must not be run away with by the suggestions of your own narrow-sighted reason. Solomon himself, the wisest of men, was so deeply versed in the doctrine of inscrutable predestination as to leave this humbling maxim on record : " When I applied my heart to know wisdom, and to see the business that is done upon the earth, then I beheld all the work of God, that a man cannot find out the work that is done under the sun, because though a man labour to seek it out, yet he shall not find it. yea, farther, though a wise man think to know it, yet shall he not be able to find it " (Eccles. viii. 16, 17).

Melancthon prosecutes the argument much further, but this may suffice for a specimen ; and it is not unworthy of notice that Luther so highly approved of Melancthon's performance, and especially of the first chapter (from whence the above extract is given), that he (Luther) thus writes of it in his epistle to Erasmus, prefixed to his book " De Serv. Arb.," " That it was worthy of everlasting duration, and to be received into the ecclesiastical canon." Let it likewise be observed that Melancthon never, to the very last, retracted a word of what he there delivers, which a person of his piety and integrity would most certainly have done had he afterwards (as some have artfully and falsely insinuated) found reason to change his judgment on these heads.

AN APPENDIX

CONCERNING THE

"FATE" OF THE ANCIENTS.

FROM THE LATIN OF JUSTUS LIPSIUS.*

FATE (says Apuleius), according to Plato, is that, "*Per quod, inevitabiles cogitationes Dei atque incepta complentur,*" whereby the purposes and designs of God are accomplished. Hence the Platonics considered providence under a threefold distinction : (1) The *providentia prima,* or that which gave birth to all effects, and is defined, by them, to be τον πρωτον θεον νοησις the intention or will of the supreme God. (2) The *providentia secunda,* or actual agency of the secondary or inferior beings, who were supposed to pervade the heavens, and from thence, by their influence, to regulate and dispose of all sublunary things, and especially to prevent the extinction of any one species below. (3) The *providentia tertia,* supposed to be exerted by the genii, whose office it was to exercise a particular care over mankind : to guard our persons and direct our actions.

But the *stoical* view of providence, or fate, was abundantly more simple, and required no such nicety of distinction. These philosophers did, at once, derive all the chain of causes and effects from their true and undoubted source, the *will* of the one living and true God. Hence, with these sages, the words Deity, Fate and Providence were frequently reciprocated as terms synonymous. Thus Seneca, speaking of God : " Will you call Him fate? You will call Him rightly, for all things are suspended on Him. Himself is *causa causarum,* the cause of all causes beside." The laws of the universe are from God, whence the same philosopher elsewhere observes, "*Omnia certa et in æternum dicta lege decurrere*": "all things

---

* Vide Lipsii Physiolog. Stoic. Lib. i. Dissert. 12.

go on according to a certain rule or decree, ordained for
ever," meaning the law of fate. So Cicero, "All things
come to pass according to the sovereignty of the eternal
law," and Pindar, probably, had an eye to this where he
says, "Νομου παντων βασιλεα, θνατων τε κια αθανατων, ειναι."
" That the law ruleth all, whether gods or mortals."
Manlius most certainly had :

> " Sed nihil in tota magis est mirabile mole,
> Quam ratio et certis quod legibus omnia parent."

Where by *ratio* is evidently meant the decreeing mind of
God, and by *leges* is meant fate, or that series of causes
and effects which is the offspring of His decree.

Homer cannot begin his " Iliad " without asserting
this grand truth, Διος δετελειετο Βουλη : " The counsel or
decree of Jupiter was fulfilled." The Divine poet sets out
on this exalted principle : he puts it in front of the noblest
poem in the world, as a testimony both of his wisdom
and his faith. It was as if he had said, " I shall sing of
numberless events, equally grand, entertaining and important, but I cannot begin to unfold them without laying down this, as a first fundamental axiom, that though
brought to pass by the instrumental agency of men, they
were the fruit of God's determining will, and of His all-
directing providence."

Neither are those minuter events, which, seemingly,
are the result of chance, excluded from this law. Even
these do not *happen*, but *come to pass* in a regular order
of succession, and at their due period of time. "*Causa
pendet ex causa : privata ac publica longus ordo rerum
trahit*," says Seneca : " Cause proceeds from cause : the
long train of things draws with it all events, both public
and private." Excellent is that of Sophocles (Aj.
Flagell.) : " I am firmly of opinion that all these things,
and whatever else befall us, are in consequence of the
Divine purpose ; whoso thinks otherwise is at liberty to
follow his own judgment, but this will ever be mine."

The *Longus ordo rerum*, mentioned by Seneca, is what he elsewhere styles *Causarum implexa series*, or a perpetual implication of causes. This, according to Laertius, was called by the stoics αιτια των οντων ειρομενη, an involved or concatenate causality of whatever has any existence, for ειρμος is a chain or implicate connection. Agreeably to this idea, Chrysippus gives the following definition of fate : " Fate is that natural, established order and constitution of all things from everlasting, whereby they mutually follow upon each other in consequence of an immutable and perpetual complication."

Let us examine this celebrated definition of fate.

(1) He calls it a *natural* συνταξις : meaning by *nature* the great *Natura Prima*, or God ; for, by some stoics, *God* and *nature* are used promiscuously. But because the Deity must be supposed both to decree and to act with wisdom, intelligence and design, fate is sometimes mentioned by them under the name of Λογος or reason. Thus they define fate (Laert. in Zen.) to be that supreme reason whereby the world is governed and directed ; or, more minutely, thus : that reason, whereby the things that have been, were ; the things that now are, have a present existence ; and the things that are to be shall be. Reason, you see, or wisdom, in the Deity, is an antecedent cause, from whence both providence and inferior nature are derived. It is added, in Strobæus, that Chrysippus sometimes varies his terms, and, instead of the word reason, substitutes the words truth, cause, nature, necessity, intimating that fate is the true, natural, necessary cause of all things that are, and of the manner in which they are.

(2) This fate is said to be εξ αιδιου, from everlasting. Nor improperly, since the constitution of things was settled and fixed in the Divine mind (where they had a sort of ideal existence) previous to their actual creation. and therefore considered as certainly future, in His decree, may be said to have been, in some sense, co-eternal with Himself.

(3) The immutable and perpetual complication mentioned in the definition means no more than that reciprocal involution of causes and effects from God downwards, by which things and events (*positis omnibus
ponendis*) are necessarily produced, according to the plan
which infinite wisdom designed from the beginning. God,
the First Cause, hath given being and activity to an
immense number of secondary subaltern causes, which
are so inseparably linked and interwoven with their
respective effects (a connection truly admirable, and not
to be comprehended by man in his present state) that
those things which do, in reality, come to pass necessarily
and by inevitable destiny, seem, to the superficial ob-
server, to come to pass in the common course of nature,
or by virtue of human reasoning and freedom. This is
that inscrutable method of Divine wisdom, "*A qua* (says
St. Augustine) *est omnis modus, omnis species, omnis
ordo, mensura, numerus, pondus; a qua sunt semina
formarum, formæ seminum, motus seminum atque
formarum.*"

Necessity is the consequence of fate. So Trismegistus :
"All things are brought about by nature and by fate,
neither is any place void of providence. Now providence
is the self-perfect reason of the super-celestial God, from
which reason of His issue two native powers, necessity
and fate." Thus, in the judgment of the wiser heathens,
effects were to be traced up to their producing causes ;
those producing causes were to be farther traced up to the
still higher causes, by which they were produced, and
those higher causes to God, the cause of *them.* Persons,
things, circumstances, events and consequences are the
effects of *necessity ;* necessity is the daughter of *fate ;* fate
is the offspring of God's infinite *wisdom* and sovereign
will. Thus, all things are ultimately resolved into their
great primary Cause, by Whom the chain was originally
let down from heaven, and on whom every link depends.

It must be owned that all the fatalists of antiquity
(particularly among the Stoics) did not constantly express
themselves with due precision. A Christian, who is

L

savingly taught by the Word and Spirit of God, must be
pained and disgusted, not to say shocked, when he reads
such an assertion as this : Την πεπρωμενην μοιραν αδυνατον
εστιν αποφυγειν και Θεω. " God Himself cannot possibly avoid
His destiny " (Herodot. 1), or that of the poet Philemon :

> "Δουλοι βασιλεων εισιν, οι βασιλεις Θεων,
> Ο Θεος αναγκης."

" Common men are servants to kings, kings are servants
to the gods, and God is a servant to necessity." So
Seneca : "*Eadem necessitas et Deos alligat: irrevocabilis
Divina pariter atque humana cursus vehit. Ille ipse,
omnium conditor ac rector, scripsit quidem Fata, sed
sequitur. Semper paret: Semel jussit.*" " The self-same
necessity binds the gods themselves. All things, Divine
as well as human, are carried forward by one identical
and overpowering rapidity. The supreme Author and
Governor of the universe hath indeed written and ordained
the fates, but, having once ordained them, He ever after
obeys them. He commanded them at first, for once, but
His conformity to them is perpetual." This is, without
doubt, very irreverently and very incautiously expressed.
Whence it has been common with many Christian writers
to tax the Stoics with setting up a first cause superior to
God Himself, and on which He is dependant.

But I apprehend these philosophers meant, in reality,
no such thing. All they designed to inculcate was that
the *will* of God and His *decrees* are *unchangeable*: that
there can be no alteration in the *Divine intention*, no new
act arise in His *mind*, no reversion of His eternal plan,
all being founded in adorable *sovereignty*, ordered by infallible *wisdom*, ratified by *omnipotence*, and cemented
with *immutability*. Thus Lucan :

> Finxit in æternum causas; qua cuncta coercet,
> Se quoque lege tenens.

And this, not through any imbecility in God or as if He
was subject to fate, of which (on the contrary) Himself
was the Ordainer, but because it is His pleasure to abide
by His own decree. For, as Seneca observes, "*Immi-*

nutio majestatis sit, et confessio erroris, mutanda fecisse.
Necesse est ei eadem placere, cui nisi optima placere non
possunt": " It would detract from the greatness of God,
and look as if He acknowledged Himself liable to mis-
takes, were He to make changeable decrees : His pleasure
must necessarily be always the same, seeing that only
which is best can, at any time, please an all-perfect
Being." A good man (adds this philosopher) is under a
kind of pleasing necessity to do good, and if he did not
do it he could not be a good man.

"*Magnum hoc argumentum est firmæ voluntatis, ne*
mutare quidem posse " : " It is a striking proof of a mag-
nanimous will to be absolutely incapable of changing."
And such is the will of God : it never fluctuates nor varies.
But, on the other hand, were He susceptible of change,
could He, through the intervention of any inferior cause
or by some untoward combination of external circumstances, be induced to recede from His purpose and alter
His plan ; it would be a most incontestible mark of weakness and dependence, the force of which argument made
Seneca, though a heathen, cry out, "*Non externa Deos*
cogunt; sed sua illis in legem æterna voluntas est":
"Outward things cannot compel the gods, but their own
eternal will is a law to themselves." It may be objected
that this seems to infer as if the Deity was still under
some kind of restraint. By no means. Let Seneca
obviate this cavil, as he effectually does, in these admirable words : " *Nec Deus ab hoc minus liber aut potens*
est; ipse enim est necessitas sua." " God is not hereby
either less free or less powerful, *for He Himself is His*
own necessity."

On the whole, it is evident that when the Stoics speak
even in the strongest terms of the obligation of fate on
God Himself, they may and ought to be understood in a
sense worthy of the adorable uncreated Majesty. In thus
interpreting the doctrine of fate, as taught by the genuine
philosophers of the Portico, I have the great St. Augustine
on my side, who, after canvassing and justly rejecting

the bastard or astrological fate, thus goes on : "*At qui omnium connectionem seriemque causarum, qua fit omne quod fit, fati nomine appellant; non multum cum eis, de verbi controversia, certandum atque laborandum est: quando quidem ipsum causarum ordinem, et quandam connectionem, summi Dei tribuunt voluntati*" : *i.e.*, "But for those philosophers (meaning the Stoics) who by the word fate mean that regular chain and series of causes, to which all things that come to pass owe their immediate existence, we will not earnestly contend with these persons about a mere term, and we the rather acquiesce in their manner of expression, because they carefully ascribe this fixed succession of things, and this mutual concatenation of causes and effects, to the will of the supreme God." Augustine adds many observations of the same import, and proves from Seneca himself, as rigid a Stoic as any, that this was the doctrine and the meaning of his philosophic brethren.

Printed in the United States
39970LVS00005B/7